Eyewitness
DOG

Bloodhound

Great Dane puppies

Red fox

Skeleton of maned wolf

Australian silky terrier

Shampooed poodle

Eyewitness
DOG

Bronze Anubis,
c. 600 B.C.–A.D. 300

Australian terrier

Written by
JULIET CLUTTON-BROCK

English setter

Two Salukis

Arctic fox cub in summer coat

Beagle
tracking

DK
Dorling Kindersley

Long-haired and miniature wire-haired dachshunds

Raccoon dog in winter coat

Skull of fennec fox

DK

LONDON, NEW YORK, MUNICH,
MELBOURNE, and DELHI

Project editor Marion Dent
Art editor Jutta Kaiser-Atcherley
Senior editor Helen Parker
Senior art editor Julia Harris
Production Louise Barratt
Picture research Cynthia Hole
Special photography Jerry Young,
Alan Hills of the British Museum,
Colin Keates of the Natural History Museum

PAPERBACK EDITION
Managing editors Linda Esposito, Andrew Macintyre
Managing art editor Jane Thomas
Senior editor David John
Project art editor Joanne Little
Editor Sarah Phillips
Art editor Rebecca Johns
Production Luca Bazzoli
Picture research Harriet Mills
DTP designer Siu Yin Ho
Consultant Kim Bryan

This Eyewitness ® Guide has been conceived by Dorling Kindersley
Limited and Editions Gallimard

Hardback edition first published in Great Britain in 1991
This edition published in Great Britain in 2004
by Dorling Kindersley Limited,
80 Strand, London WC2R 0RL

2 4 6 8 10 9 7 5 3 1

Copyright © 1991, © 2004 Dorling Kindersley Limited, London
A Penguin Company

A CIP catalogue record for this book is available from the
British Library

ISBN 1 4053 0546 0
Colour reproduction by Colourscan, Singapore
Printed in China by Toppan Co., (Shenzhen) Ltd

See our complete
catalogue at

www.dk.com

Cross-bred dog

Bronze dog from Egypt,
c. 300 B.C.–A.D. 300

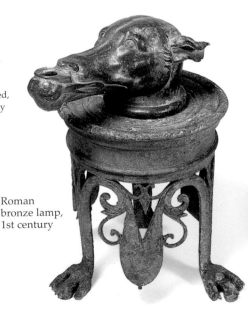

French
bulldog

Lurcher

Roman
bronze lamp,
1st century

Contents

Boxer

What is a dog?

THE DOG FAMILY, called Canidae from the Latin *canis* meaning "dog", includes around 35 species of living wolves, jackals, foxes, and wild and domestic dogs. All members of the dog family, or canids, are carnivores, or meat eaters, and have special adaptations for hunting. Their teeth (pp. 8–9) are used for killing prey, chewing meat, gnawing bones, and sometimes for fighting each other. Their highly developed senses of sight, sound, and smell (pp. 14–17) – with their large eyes, erect ears, and sensitive noses – mean they can track prey successfully, whether they are social, or solitary, hunters (pp. 18–19). All wild dogs, except for the South American bush dog (pp. 32–33), have long legs adapted for running fast in pursuit of prey. All canids are "digitigrade" (they walk on their toes), and have distinctive feet, with five claws on the front foot and four on the hind. In domestic dogs, there is sometimes an extra, fifth claw (dew claw) on the hind foot. Wild dogs have long tails, and their dense fur is usually without spots or stripes (pp. 12–13). Canids usually mate once a year and, after two months' development in the womb, produce a litter of pups (pp. 20–21). Like all mammals, the mother suckles her young after they are born and looks after them for several months, with help from the rest of the family.

DISTRIBUTION OF DOGS
Wild canids originally lived in every continent of the world, except Australasia, where they have been introduced by humans (pp. 36–37), and Antarctica.

North America

Europe

Asia

Africa

South America

Australia

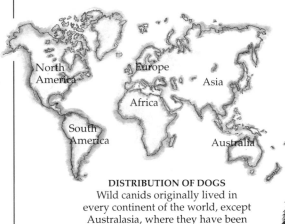

Coat is multi-coloured and distinctive

Ears are small, erect, and rounded

THE JOVIAL JACKAL
There are three species of jackal (pp. 24–25) – the golden, the side-striped, and the black-backed. They all live in Africa, but the golden jackal also lives in parts of Europe and Asia. Jackals live and hunt in pairs that usually stay together for the whole of their lives.

Golden jackal

Bushy tail, or brush

Red fox

RED SOLITAIRE
The red fox is a solitary hunter of rabbits and rodents. The behaviour of all foxes (pp. 28–31) differs from other canids (pp. 18–19). The most characteristic part of the fox is its bushy tail.

DOGGY ALL-SORTS
Dogs have been bred in an amazing assortment of shapes, sizes and colours. This painting shows just some of the 400 breeds of domestic dog (pp. 48–61) in the world. All these breeds are descended from the wolf, which was first tamed by humans about 12,000 years ago (pp. 8–9).

WARM FEET
Of the many ways dogs have helped people, one of the more unusual ones was as foot warmer for church congregations in the Middle Ages. Shown in this beautiful stained glass (right) are the biblical characters Tobias and Sarah – and their dog.

Teeth number the usual 42 (pp. 8–9), but first lower molars are small and flat – unlike other dogs' teeth

THE LARGEST CANID
The wolf (pp. 22–23) is the largest of all the wild canids. It lives and hunts in a family group, or pack, and is the most social (pp. 18–19) of all the carnivores. The wolf is the ancestor of all domestic dogs (pp. 48–61).

This wolf has thick grey fur, but the fur can vary from nearly pure white, red, or brown to black

Grey wolf

AFRICAN HUNTER
The African hunting dog is a highly developed social carnivore (pp. 18–19) that hunts in family groups. These wild dogs live in the grasslands of Africa (pp. 26–27), but are in danger of extinction from being killed in great numbers by farmers, from disease, and from prey stolen by other predators.

African hunting dog

Shorter hind legs give typical crouching position

Muzzle is heavy and teeth very different from a dog's

This striped hyena is found in Africa and western Asia. Hyenas are hunters and scavengers, with powerful teeth that crush bones that big cats are not able to chew.

Long, powerful front legs

The Tasmanian wolf looked similar to a dog, but it was a marsupial and unrelated to the dog family. It is now only known from stuffed specimens in museums.

Rounded ears

Thick, muscular base of tail could not wag like a dog's

What is not a dog?
Sometimes called dogs, the hyena, Tasmanian wolf, and prairie dog are not in the dog family. The three species of hyena, within the Hyaenidae family, are more closely related to cats. The Tasmanian wolf, or thylacine, now extinct, was a marsupial (pouched mammal) that lived in Australia, while the North American prairie dog is a rodent related to squirrels.

Prairie dogs are highly social rodents that live in communal burrows covering up to 65 ha (160 acres).

Evolution of the dog family

THIRTY MILLION YEARS AGO, during the Oligocene period, the first dog-like creature, *Cynodictis* (a mongoose-like animal with a long muzzle), appeared on Earth. It replaced the earlier widespread group of carnivores – the creodonts. All the earliest fossils of the dog family have been found in North America and date from this period. Another canid-like carnivore, *Tomarctus*, evolved during the Miocene period, from 24 million years ago. In turn the genus *Canis* evolved, which became *Canis lupus*, or wolf, some 300,000 years ago. From this wolf, the first domestic dogs date from around 12,000 years ago. There were also creatures that looked similar to these dog ancestors, such as the hyaenodonts from the Oligocene, but they were not related to true hyenas, which are closer to the cat family. From ancestral carnivores like *Cynodictis*, the canids evolved into fast-running meat eaters that hunted prey on open grasslands, and most of today's living species have inherited this way of life.

Cranium (brain box)

Nasal bone

Upper jaw bone

Orbit for eye

Ear bone

Upper carnassial tooth for tearing flesh

Foramen magnum – entrance for the spinal cord to the brain

Cranium

Upper molar

Side view of *Cynodictis* skull

Palatal bone

Orbit

Palatal view of *Cynodictis* skull

THIRTY-MILLION-YEAR-OLD HEAD
This is the fossilized skull of one of the ancestors of the dog family. It was a mongoose-like animal called *Cynodictis*, and it lived about 30 million years ago.

DIRE CONSEQUENCES
The extinct dire wolf (below) lived in California during the period of the Ice Ages. It was huge – much larger than any living wolf – and it preyed on the mammoth and other large Ice Age mammals.

Restoration of dire wolf

Reconstruction of a scene at the tar pits of Rancho La Brea near Los Angeles, California, USA, showing dire wolves and a *Smilodon* attacking a mammoth (right)

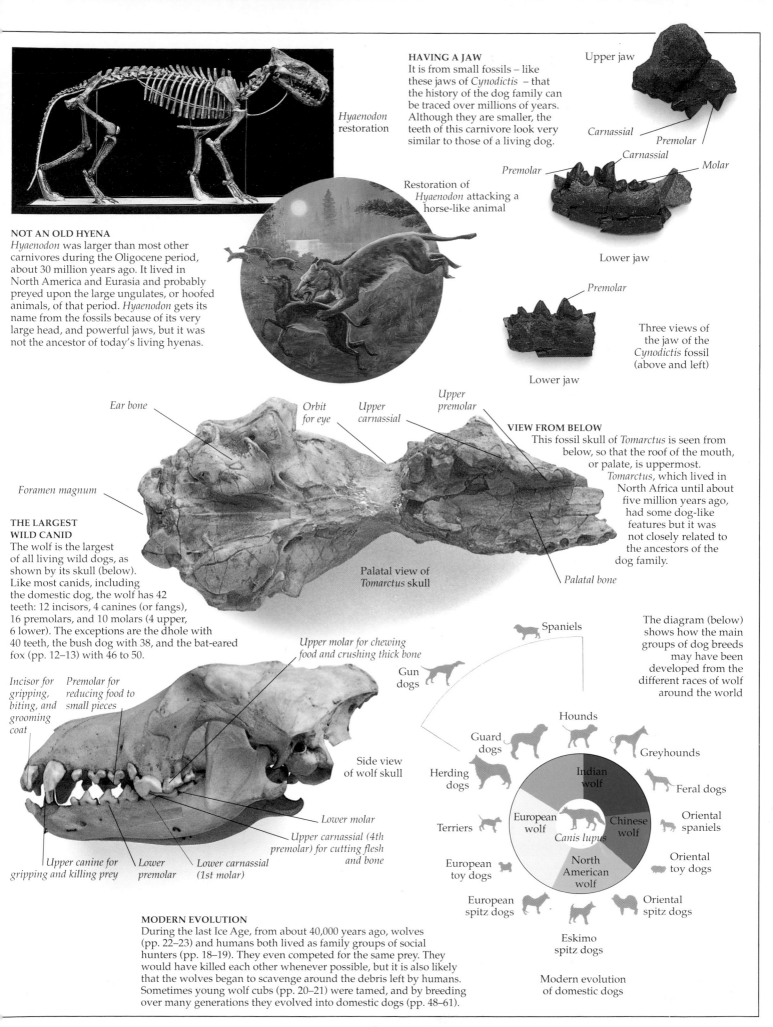

HAVING A JAW
It is from small fossils – like these jaws of *Cynodictis* – that the history of the dog family can be traced over millions of years. Although they are smaller, the teeth of this carnivore look very similar to those of a living dog.

Hyaenodon restoration

Upper jaw

Carnassial

Premolar

Carnassial

Premolar

Molar

Lower jaw

Restoration of *Hyaenodon* attacking a horse-like animal

Premolar

Three views of the jaw of the *Cynodictis* fossil (above and left)

Lower jaw

NOT AN OLD HYENA
Hyaenodon was larger than most other carnivores during the Oligocene period, about 30 million years ago. It lived in North America and Eurasia and probably preyed upon the large ungulates, or hoofed animals, of that period. *Hyaenodon* gets its name from the fossils because of its very large head, and powerful jaws, but it was not the ancestor of today's living hyenas.

Ear bone

Orbit for eye

Upper carnassial

Upper premolar

VIEW FROM BELOW
This fossil skull of *Tomarctus* is seen from below, so that the roof of the mouth, or palate, is uppermost. *Tomarctus*, which lived in North Africa until about five million years ago, had some dog-like features but it was not closely related to the ancestors of the dog family.

Foramen magnum

THE LARGEST WILD CANID
The wolf is the largest of all living wild dogs, as shown by its skull (below). Like most canids, including the domestic dog, the wolf has 42 teeth: 12 incisors, 4 canines (or fangs), 16 premolars, and 10 molars (4 upper, 6 lower). The exceptions are the dhole with 40 teeth, the bush dog with 38, and the bat-eared fox (pp. 12–13) with 46 to 50.

Palatal view of *Tomarctus* skull

Palatal bone

Upper molar for chewing food and crushing thick bone

Spaniels

The diagram (below) shows how the main groups of dog breeds may have been developed from the different races of wolf around the world

Gun dogs

Incisor for gripping, biting, and grooming coat

Premolar for reducing food to small pieces

Hounds

Guard dogs

Greyhounds

Herding dogs

Indian wolf

Feral dogs

Side view of wolf skull

Terriers

European wolf

Chinese wolf

Canis lupus

Oriental spaniels

Lower molar

Upper carnassial (4th premolar) for cutting flesh and bone

European toy dogs

North American wolf

Oriental toy dogs

Upper canine for gripping and killing prey

Lower premolar

Lower carnassial (1st molar)

European spitz dogs

Oriental spitz dogs

Eskimo spitz dogs

Modern evolution of domestic dogs

MODERN EVOLUTION
During the last Ice Age, from about 40,000 years ago, wolves (pp. 22–23) and humans both lived as family groups of social hunters (pp. 18–19). They even competed for the same prey. They would have killed each other whenever possible, but it is also likely that the wolves began to scavenge around the debris left by humans. Sometimes young wolf cubs (pp. 20–21) were tamed, and by breeding over many generations they evolved into domestic dogs (pp. 48–61).

Dogs' bones

THE SKELETONS OF ALL MAMMALS provide the solid framework on which the rest of the body is built. The bones of the skull protect the brain, mouth, eyes, nose, and ears. The backbone supports the heart, lungs, and digestive system. The shoulder blade and hip girdle are the pivots which allow the limb bones to move. Attached to the ends of the bones, there are ligaments and tendons which act like strong elastic to keep them joined together yet moveable. Muscles are also attached to the bones in a complicated system that enables the body to move in all directions. Each bone in the skeleton has characteristics which make it recognizable as belonging to a member of the dog family. The skulls of wolves, dogs (both wild and domestic), and foxes are always long and the teeth large. The neck and the backbone are also relatively long, the ribs form a strong cage to protect the chest, and the long limb bones are adapted for fast running.

OLD MOTHER HUBBARD
This familiar nursery rhyme crone has no bones for her dog to chew (pp. 62–63) – "her cupboard is bare".

Skull of a wolf can always be recognized by the large size of the tearing, or carnassial, tooth

LARGE AS LIFE
Apart from some giant domestic dogs, the wolf (pp. 22–23) has the largest skeleton of all the animals in the dog family.

Arctic wolf

Neck vertebrae

Sternum

Elbow joint

Radius

Ulna

AFRICAN HUNTER
The African hunting dog (pp. 26–27) has very long legs in relation to the size of its body, so it is able to range over huge distances in search of prey.

African hunting dog

Skeleton of African hunting dog

Pelvis

Tibia

Radius

Elbow joint

Ulna

Ankle joint, or hock

Red fox

LITTLE RED
The red fox spends much of its time creeping under bushes and rocks. It has shorter legs, compared to the size of its body, than the wolf.

Skeleton of red fox

Lower jaw

Shoulder joint

Sternum

Metacarpal bone

Skeleton of Maltese dog

BALL OF FLUFF
This fluffy Maltese dog does not look at all like a wolf, but inside its skin the skeleton is just like that of a tiny wolf.

Round skull

Neck is short, but still has seven vertebrae

Maltese dog

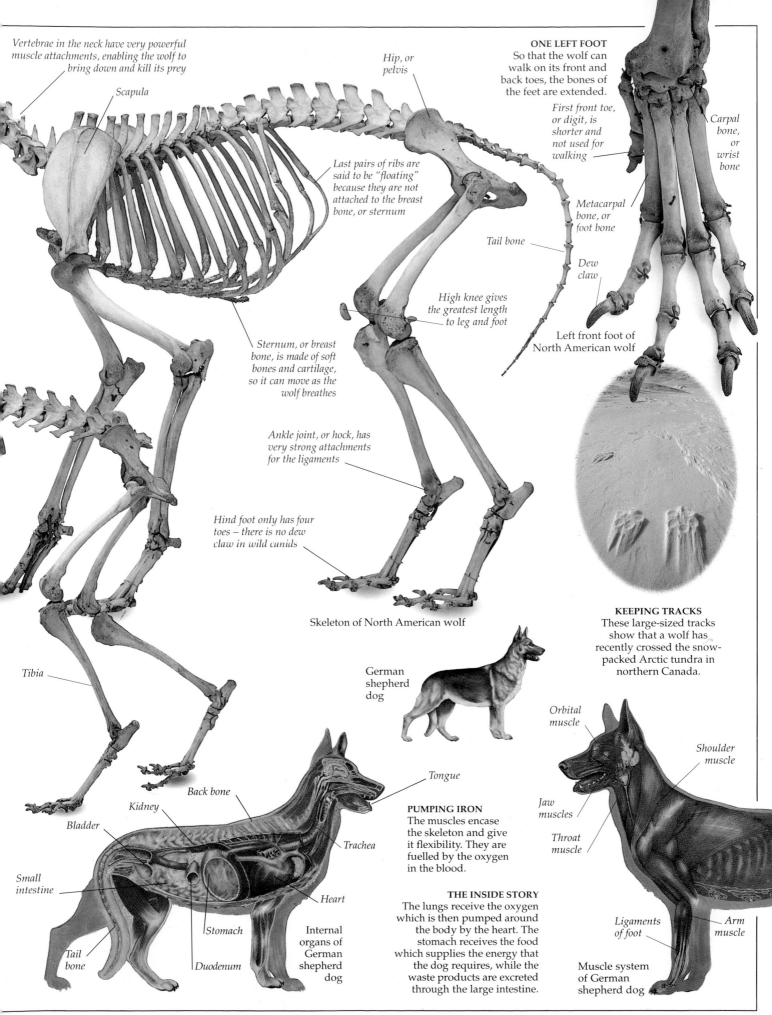

Vertebrae in the neck have very powerful muscle attachments, enabling the wolf to bring down and kill its prey

Scapula

Hip, or pelvis

ONE LEFT FOOT
So that the wolf can walk on its front and back toes, the bones of the feet are extended.

First front toe, or digit, is shorter and not used for walking

Carpal bone, or wrist bone

Last pairs of ribs are said to be "floating" because they are not attached to the breast bone, or sternum

Metacarpal bone, or foot bone

Tail bone

Dew claw

High knee gives the greatest length to leg and foot

Left front foot of North American wolf

Sternum, or breast bone, is made of soft bones and cartilage, so it can move as the wolf breathes

Ankle joint, or hock, has very strong attachments for the ligaments

Hind foot only has four toes – there is no dew claw in wild canids

Tibia

Skeleton of North American wolf

German shepherd dog

KEEPING TRACKS
These large-sized tracks show that a wolf has recently crossed the snow-packed Arctic tundra in northern Canada.

Back bone

Kidney

Tongue

Bladder

Trachea

Small intestine

Heart

Stomach

Tail bone

Duodenum

Internal organs of German shepherd dog

PUMPING IRON
The muscles encase the skeleton and give it flexibility. They are fuelled by the oxygen in the blood.

THE INSIDE STORY
The lungs receive the oxygen which is then pumped around the body by the heart. The stomach receives the food which supplies the energy that the dog requires, while the waste products are excreted through the large intestine.

Orbital muscle

Shoulder muscle

Jaw muscles

Throat muscle

Ligaments of foot

Arm muscle

Muscle system of German shepherd dog

Coats, heads, and tails

I<small>N THE DOG FAMILY</small>, fur has many different lengths and textures. Fur is necessary to keep dogs warm, being denser in cold climates, but shorter in hot ones. It is composed of two layers: an undercoat of fine wool, usually of one colour; and a top coat of longer, coarser hairs, called guard hairs, which have natural oils to make the coat waterproof, and carry the stripy, or brindled, pattern of the fur. Coat colours are variations of white, black, and tan. The heads of all wild dogs, whether large like the wolf, or small like the bat-eared fox, have long heads with erect ears, and teeth set in a line along straight jaws. Tails too are all similar, being long, straight, often bushy, with a white or black tip. A dog's tail is one of its most important assets and is used for balancing when running fast, for expressing its feelings, and, when held up, as a signal to other members of its group. No wild dog has a tail permanently curled over its back. When dogs were domesticated, all these characteristics were altered by specially selecting certain features for each dog breed.

FUR COATS
Before the present century, for people to keep warm in the winter, it was essential to have clothing made from animal furs. Today, with all the artificial materials available, wearing a fur coat shows that the person has no regard for the dwindling numbers of wild animals and no compassion for their suffering.

Tails of many domestic dogs – like this Australian terrier (pp. 52–53) – are docked so that the tail stands up straight

Tail of the red fox (pp. 28–29) is always reddish and bushy, and is referred to as a brush

Thick tail of Bernese mountain dog (pp. 56–57) keeps it warm

Grey tree fox (pp. 28–29) has typically soft grey fur (left)

Sand fox (pp. 30-31) lives in very hot places and has fine, dense fur (above)

African hunting dog (pp. 26–27) has short hair (above) so it does not get too hot when running

Wire-hair of a miniature dachshund (above)

Dachshunds (pp. 48–49) can be long-haired (right), short-haired, or wire-haired (far right)

Dalmatian's (pp. 54–55) tail even has spots on it

Hairy tail of giant Schnauzer is cut short by docking (pp. 44–45)

LOSING THEIR HAIR
Most wild and domestic dogs moult every spring and autumn, so they have a thin coat in the summer and a thick one in the winter. The fur of this German shepherd dog (pp. 44–45) is moulting.

Brain case
(cranium)

Large orbit for eye

Incisor tooth

Huge
head

DOGS' ANCESTOR
Wolves (pp. 22–23)
have typical long
heads and
muzzles.

Canine tooth

Side view of skull
of Japanese Chin

Lower jaw

A JAPANESE CHIN
All dogs are descended
from wolves, even this
Japanese Chin, or
spaniel, with its little
round head and
short curved jaws.

Carnassial

Canine
tooth

Incisor

Arctic wolf

Powerful
nose

Hard palate

Ear bone

Zygomatic, or bony,
arch at outside edge
of eye socket

Palatal view
(showing roof of
mouth) of skull
of Japanese Chin

DOG SLEUTH
The bloodhound has a
straight head, but not a
pronounced muzzle, and
uses its powerful sense of
smell for tracking (pp. 16–17).

Palatal view
(showing roof of mouth)
of bat-eared fox

Small molar for
eating insects

Bloodhound

Straight
profile
to head

DIFFERENT TEETH
The bat-eared fox has
teeth that are different from
any other canid (they are smaller
and there are 4 to 8 more than the
usual 42) but its head is still dog-like.

Incisor

Hard palate

Fox terrier

STRAIGHT-LACED
The fox terrier (pp. 52–53)
has been bred to have a
very straight head, with
no angle between the
brain case and the face.

Brain case
(cranium)

Zygomatic, or bony,
arch of eye socket

Nasal
region

Pekingese

Ear
bone

Flat face

Incisor

Side view of skull
of bat-eared fox

Lower jaw

Canine
tooth

PERKY PEKE
Years of selective
breeding (pp. 58–59)
have given the Pekingese a
small, round head, flat face,
floppy ears, and soft fur.

Sight and sound

LISTENING DOG
The large erect ears are turned this way and that as this dog works out where the sounds it is listening to are coming from.

EVERY DOMESTIC DOG IN THE WORLD, whether it is a Pekingese (pp. 58–59) or a Great Dane (pp. 56–57), has inherited the eyes and ears of its ancestor, the wolf. All its senses have evolved for being a social hunter of large prey, but these senses have been adapted and developed in different breeds of dog by "artificial selection". This means, for example, that in sight hounds (pp. 48–49), such as greyhounds, those puppies with particularly good sight have been chosen over the centuries as future breeders, so that in the course of time all greyhounds have developed even better sight than the wolf. One change that has been brought about in nearly all domestic dogs is that the eyes look forward rather than to the side, as in the wolf. Wolves and domestic dogs cannot hear as well as some other carnivores, because they usually hunt at dusk when sight is more important than hearing. Foxes, however, hunt at night and it is thought that their sense of hearing is more acute than a wolf's.

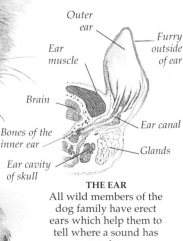

HUNTING HORN
Hunting dogs are trained to follow the sound of a horn as well as the human voice.

DOG'S WHISTLE
Most dogs will respond to the sound of a whistle.

Dense fur keeps the fennec warm on cold nights in the desert

FENNEC FOX
The fennec is the smallest member of the fox family. It lives in the deserts of the Sahara and Arabia and is well adapted for keeping cool and finding any food it can in the hot, dry sand.

The fennec's light-coloured fur is pale to reflect the heat of the desert during the day

Huge ears help the fennec to keep cool and to hear the slightest sound – which could mean that its next meal is nearby

Outer ear

Furry outside of ear

Ear muscle

Brain

Ear canal

Bones of the inner ear

Glands

Ear cavity of skull

THE EAR
All wild members of the dog family have erect ears which help them to tell where a sound has come from.

The belly fur is even paler, as it is on nearly every carnivore

BEAUTIFUL BORZOI
The borzoi (pp. 46–47) is a typical sight, or "gaze", hound. Because of its keen sight it was used in the Middle East for game hunting, and later by Russian royalty in traditional wolf-hunts.

The eyes are large and face well forwards so the borzoi probably has stereoscopic vision, which means that it can see in three dimensions like humans

Upper eyelid

Pupil

Iris

Lower eyelid

Third eyelid, or nictitating membrane

THE EYE
Inside a dog's upper and lower eyelids, there is a third eyelid – which protects the eye from dirt and dust.

JACKAL-HEADED GOD OF MUMMIFICATION
Anubis, a jackal-headed god in ancient Egypt, supervised embalming and weighed the hearts of the dead.

Muzzles (pp. 46–47) are usually worn by racing greyhounds

When the upper teeth closely overlap the lower teeth, it is called a scissor bite

A WINNING GREYHOUND
This greyhound is waiting intently for the start of the race and all its senses are directed forwards. As it races it will keep its eyes centred on the mechanical hare as though it were a live animal.

MANED WOLF
The so-called "maned wolf" (pp. 32–33) of the South American savanna has very large ears for hearing the slightest sound in the long grass.

Dog collar

THE CHASE IS ON
This pack of African hunting dogs is chasing a gemsbok. They use their big eyes to see their prey and their large ears to hear the communicating sounds of the pack, and also to hear whether any other predators are trying to take over their prey.

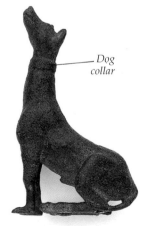

GUARD DOG
This dog – an ancient Roman sculpture – is anxiously watching and listening for any thieves at the door.

On the scent trail

ALL MEMBERS OF THE CANID OR DOG FAMILY have a far better sense of smell than any human, and they probably remember scents better than sights. That is to say, whereas humans remember how objects are placed in a room and what they look like, a dog will remember the arrangement of the objects by their different scents. In all wild canids – wolves, wild dogs, jackals, and foxes – smell is the most highly developed of all the senses. The animal hunts with its nose, finds its mate with its nose, and identifies every new being that comes into its territory with its nose. It can even tell whether other animals are relaxed or afraid by their smell. This acute perception of scent is made possible by the long nose of the skull which contains rolls of very thin bone over which the particles of scent are drawn. With certain hunting and gun dogs, there has been selection for the sense of smell in preference to the other senses. These dogs, such as the bloodhound, can smell very well but are short-sighted.

WHO ARE YOU?
A dog can learn a lot about another dog by smelling the anal gland just beneath its tail.

Drop ears in scent hounds mean that their hearing is not as good as that of a wild dog, or fox, with erect ears

Saluki

Dalmatian

TRUFFLE HUNTING
A truffle is a fungus that grows underground and is considered to be a great food delicacy, especially in France where dogs are trained to search for truffles by their smell.

A nose, close to the ground, picks up any scents of prey

ATTACKING
ormally, a fox would not attack a sheep but it might do so if it could smell that the sheep was already dying. Foxes do kill lambs.

NASAL CAVITY
A dog's keen sense of smell is due to rolls of very fine bone, or turbinals, in its nasal cavity. These are connected to a fine mesh of nerve endings joining up with the olfactory nerve which takes scent messages to the brain.

Nasal cavity with paper-thin turbinal bones

Sinuses

Cavity of brain

Fleshy nose

Lip

Palate

MINI DACHSHUND'S NOSE
Like all the dog family, this miniature dachshund has a leathery nose and two nostrils through which scents are drawn into the nasal cavity.

The bat-eared fox's keen sense of smell allows it to find its prey quickly

BAT-EARED FOX
The bat-eared fox eats any small animal or fruit that it can find, and it needs a keen sense of smell to find beetles underground.

Strong legs and excellent stamina make the beagle a dependable hunter

BEAGLE
Scent hounds, like this beagle, have been bred to use their noses more than their eyes and ears in the hunt. Because of this well-developed sense of smell, they can pursue small game very successfully. With less keen hearing the dog can concentrate on tracking a scent without being distracted by slight noises.

Looking for prey . . .

. . . and finding a surprise

ENGLISH SETTER
Like the pointer, the setters are scent hounds. They are trained to "set up" game birds from the ground so they can be shot in the air.

Behaviour

BEHAVIOUR IN THE DOG family is divided into two distinct groups of solitary hunters, and social hunters. The solitary hunters – that is, the foxes and South American wild dogs (pp. 28–33) – live on their own, except when they are mating and rearing their young. The wolf, jackal, coyote, African hunting dog, dhole (pp. 22–27), and the domestic dog (pp. 14–17), are all social hunters. Their behaviour is in many ways like that of a human family in which the parents are the leaders, while the children should do as they are told until they are old enough to leave and form their own family groups. In a wolf pack, or a family of African hunting dogs, every individual knows which other dog is above or below it in the family hierarchy and it will fight hard to keep or to better its position. Even though wolves are such powerful killers, fights between them seldom end in death, and if one wolf is injured the others will often help it to feed.

Ears back show dog is afraid – or even potentially aggressive

Dog appears happy and relaxed – with pert ears and smiling mouth

Cross-bred dog

GETTING TO KNOW YOU
The strong, dominant wolf on the left is greeting the weaker, more submissive wolf on the right.

Ears laid back show fear, or aggression

Tail between legs shows dog in a submissive stance

Mouth shut tightly denotes apprehension

German shepherd dog

BODY LANGUAGE
Even though dogs cannot speak like humans they can say all they need to each other by the postures of their bodies and tails.

JUST GOOD FRIENDS
This charming painting by English artist John Charlton (1849–1917), shows three dogs of indistinct breeds (pp. 60–61) playing together in the snow and exhibiting their friendly relationship with one another.

Crouched body means fox is waiting to pounce

Alert ears show fox is listening out for potential prey

Solitary hunters

Foxes, including this American grey fox (pp. 28–29), are solitary hunters that kill their prey by themselves. They do not, therefore, have the complicated, interactive behaviour of the social hunters. A fox's tail cannot wag as expressively as a wolf's and its upright ears are not so mobile. Even so, if a fox is frightened it will cower down to make itself look small, and if it is angry it will stand up as tall as it can to look large and threatening.

Grey, or tree, fox

Social hunters

The African hunting dog and other social hunters not only have to provide enough meat for the family group but they must also defend themselves against other large predators, like the big cats and the hyena. However, human hunters have always been the main competitors of the social hunters. The wolf (pp. 22–23) has been exterminated over much of its vast range in Europe and Asia, and the African hunting dog and the dhole (pp. 26–27) are also near to extinction. Only the jackals and the coyote (pp. 24–25), being smaller and more adaptable, continue to flourish.

Two wolves fighting it out to see which one will be the leader

HOWLIN' WOLVES
Like its wolf ancestors, this pointer will howl if left on its own in an effort to communicate with others of its kind. Some dogs will also howl when they hear certain kinds of music.

TOP DOG
Although much smaller than the Dalmatian, this Norfolk terrier has the stronger personality and is showing that he is top dog.

Dalmatian's head is slightly turned away, showing fear

Norfolk terrier's positive stance shows his confidence towards the larger dog

Dalmatian

Norfolk terrier

FIGHTING FOR A BITE
At a kill, these African hunting dogs will eat vast quantities of meat which is later vomited up, or regurgitated, for their young, or for other members of the pack, who will fight over these half-digested morsels.

Pointer

DOGS' SOCIAL CLUB
This caricature by J. J. Granville, published in Paris, France, in 1859, emphasizes the similarity of dog behaviour with that of humans.

Cubs and puppies

Four-week-old Great Dane puppies. . .

THE YOUNG OF ALL MEMBERS of the dog family (Canidae) look quite similar when they are new born. They are small, defenceless, blind, and short-haired, with short legs and a little tail. At first, like all mammals, the cubs or puppies, which may vary in number from one to twelve or more, can only suck milk from their mother. After a few days (about nine in the domestic dog) their eyes open, they begin to hear, and they soon need more solid food. This is provided by the mother, and in social species by other members of the group who vomit up (regurgitate) meat that they have previously eaten. A mother dog who looks as though she is being sick in front of her puppies is, therefore, not ill but is providing them with their first solid meal. In the wild the young are nearly always born in a den or hole in the ground, and in the same way a domestic dog needs a dark, warm place where she can give birth, which will happen about 63 days after she has been mated.

FOOD FOR THOUGHT
This mother fox is bringing home a rabbit for her three cubs, who are hungrily awaiting food in their den.

. . .playfully attacking each other. . .

IT'S PLAYTIME
It is essential that all puppies should be allowed space in which to play. They must have exercise in order to grow properly, but – of equal importance – is their need to learn social interaction with other dogs and with humans. In this playing sequence, two Great Dane puppies (aged four weeks) are learning to relate to one another.

. . .with one trying to dominate the other

All is well – they're friends again

LOOKING ENDEARING
The puppies of a Great Dane (above and right) are no different in their needs from a Pekingese or a wolf. Although, as they are the giants amongst dogs, they require a great deal of wholesome meat, extra calcium as well as vitamins, and large bones to chew (pp. 62–63). They also need a great deal of space in which to play and exercise their growing limbs.

Six-week-old Great Dane puppies

NURSING MOTHER
This mother wolf is contentedly suckling her cubs, but in a few weeks their sharp little milk teeth will have grown and will hurt her nipples. Then she will begin to wean the cubs with regurgitated meat.

LEARNING TO BEHAVE
The play of these African hunting dog pups is a school for adult life in which they must be powerful hunters. Just as with the Great Dane puppies, they learn the rules of social behaviour from their games.

A small bronze Greek sculpture of a pregnant bitch – from the fifth century B.C.

Four-and-a-half-months-old black Labrador puppy

Dalmatian at six months

A TAIL OF TWO PUPPIES
These puppies are having a tussle. The Dalmatian is a little older than the black Labrador and he is the dominant dog. They are both about half-grown and in a few months they could be fighting in earnest.

GETTING CARRIED AWAY
All members of the dog family will carry their cubs about. Usually, it is the mother but, sometimes, the father will also take the cub, gently by the scruff of its neck with his teeth, and carry it to safety.

WOLF-BOYS
Legend has it that the city of Rome in Italy was founded in 753 B.C. by two brothers – Romulus and Remus – who had been suckled as babies by a she-wolf.

Leader of the pack

THE WOLF PACK is very like a human family group, in which the oldest male and the oldest female are the leaders, and the young must do as they are told. Wolves and humans have many patterns of social behaviour in common, for both evolved as social hunters who had to keep together in a team so they could kill animals larger than themselves. Wolves guard their territory closely and make their presence known by howling (pp. 18–19). Each member of the pack knows his or her position in the scale of dominance, and any wolf that tries to assert itself is likely to be expelled from the pack by the leaders. The only pair of wolves to mate are the dominant male and the dominant female, and after the cubs are born the father will bring meat back to the den for the mother. The cubs are suckled for about ten weeks, and then the mother and the younger wolves will feed them with regurgitated meat (partly digested meat returned to the mouth from the stomach) until they are old enough to start hunting with the pack. At first, the young cubs can behave as they like and all the wolves will put up with their play-fights, but as they grow older they too must learn to keep their place.

FOLLOW THE LEADER
This group of European wolves is following its leader on the way to look for prey in the forest. They will eat anything they can find – from an elk to a mouse – and if food is really scarce they will even eat insects and berries. Wolves will range over a huge area, up to 1,000 sq km (400 sq miles), in packs that can be as large as 20 individuals.

Ears are erect to show that the wolf is on the alert – either for prey or foe

EUROPEAN GREY WOLF
In earlier times there were wolves in every country of Europe but they have been slaughtered by farmers and hunters for hundreds of years and are now found only in southern and eastern Europe and on the borders of Norway and Sweden.

Sharp teeth enable wolf to kill its prey quickly

A WOLF OF MANY COLOURS
The Arctic wolf from the far north of Canada has a hard life trying to find prey in the freezing cold of the Arctic Circle. These wolves have a very thick, white winter coat to camouflage them in the snow and ice, although they can be shades of grey or buff, or occasionally even black during the summer. They have short tails and small ears to keep the body as compact as possible. Arctic wolves feed on hares, birds, and, sometimes, if they are lucky, a pack will be able to kill a deer or a musk ox.

LITTLE RED RIDING HOOD
When there really were wolves in the forests, mothers would have told their children the story of Little Red Riding Hood – of how she was tricked by a very clever wolf – to frighten them from going out alone.

A RARE RED WOLF
The red wolf is smaller than the grey wolf and is adapted for living in the warmer climate of the southeastern USA. It was extinct in the wild but in 1988 a few were reintroduced into North Carolina, USA.

WINNER OR LOSER
Wolves are quick to snarl at each other and they fight quite often. However, a wolf will seldom be killed in a fight, although it can be seriously hurt.

TROUBLE AHEAD FOR BRAVE NOVICE
According to the legends of the Nootka Indians in northwest America, novices were sometimes carried away by wolves. This club may have been used as a display object to represent the powers the brave received during his captivity. Made of abalone shell, bone, and human hair, a wolf's head is carved at one end.

The legs have to be long and very powerful so the wolf can range over huge distances in search of prey

ETHIOPIAN HOWLER
The Ethiopian wolf is in danger of extinction because the high grassland plains where it lives are being increasingly taken over by farmers for livestock grazing. There may only be about 500 of these distinctive tawny-red wolves left in the wild.

MAKING A MEAL OF IT
A pack of wolves chase musk oxen on Ellesmere Island in the Arctic in the hope of finding food.

The tail of this wolf is pointing down, showing it is rather wary of what is ahead

Jackals and coyotes

Limestone stele of Egyptian, kneeling before the jackal of Wepwawet, with 63 other jackals, made after 550 B.C.

THE JACKALS, AND THE COYOTE, which lives only in North America, come below the wolf in the scale of social hunters (pp. 18–19) – the wolf being one of the most social of all animals that hunt on land. Of the jackals, there are three species, all of which are found in Africa. The most widespread is the golden jackal, which is found in southeastern Europe and southern Asia as well as in Africa. The side-striped jackal and the black-backed jackal are both found in Africa, south of the Sahara. All the jackals, and the coyote, live in close-knit family groups that forage for any food they can find. This may vary from the carcass of an animal long since dead and left unwanted by other carnivores, to an antelope that they themselves have managed to kill. When a litter of pups is born (pp. 20–21), all the jackals in the family will help to look after them and bring back food for them to the den.

GOLDEN OLDIES
This pair of golden jackals will stay together for their whole lives, hunting and breeding together, unless one of them is killed. They will patrol their territory together, scent-mark it with their urine, and prevent any other intruding jackals from coming near.

SILVER SADDLE
This jackal has a spectacular coat of fine fur with a black, or silver, saddle. The black-backed jackal lives on open grasslands in eastern and southern Africa.

This mummified canid in the form of the jackal god, Anubis, is from ancient Egypt, between 600 B.C. and A.D. 300.

SOCIAL COYOTE
The name "coyote" comes from the Aztec word, *coyotl*. The coyote – also called a brush, or prairie, wolf – is the jackal of North America and, like the jackal, it is a social hunter (pp. 18–19) that lives in pairs and family groups.

CUNNING COYDOG
Wild coyotes sometimes mate with domestic dogs and produce "coydog" pups. As they are neither wild nor tame, coydogs have a hard time and often take to killing domestic livestock for food.

CANID QUICKSTEP
This golden jackal is doing a quick turn in its lookout for prey.

DOG DANCE
Dogs were highly regarded by native North Americans, both for their meat and for transport (pp. 56–57). This painting, by the Swiss artist Karl Bodmer (1809–1893), shows a medicine man of the Hidatsa tribe who is wearing a special costume while performing a "dog dance". The Hidatsa tribe lived along the Missouri river in North Dakota, USA.

Skull is smaller than a wolf's, with a flat forehead and comparatively small teeth

Golden jackal's coarse, short-haired coat varies in colour from pale gold to brown-tipped yellow, depending on season and region

WHITE STRIPE
The side-striped jackal lives in woodland areas in tropical Africa. Its coat is a mix of colours, including grey, tawny, white, and black. A distinctive white stripe runs along its side from elbow to hip and it has a white-tipped tail.

JACKAL WORSHIP
Anubis, the jackal god, is frequently shown in ancient Egyptian artefacts.

African and Asian dogs

THERE ARE MANY WILD DOGS living in Africa and Asia, apart from the jackals (pp. 24–25), which live on both continents, and the wolf (pp. 22–23), which lives in Asia but not Africa. In Africa there are the hunting dog (pp. 6–7) and the bat-eared fox (p. 13, p. 17), which is not a fox, and has teeth that are quite different from those of all other wild dogs. Living in India and Southeast Asia is the "red dog", or dhole, as well as the raccoon dog, which comes from eastern Asia and Japan. All these wild dogs are social hunters, while the Tibetan fox, from the high mountains of Tibet, and the Bengal fox are true foxes (pp. 28–29) and are solitary hunters (pp. 18–19) of rodents and other small animals. Each of the many species of wild dog that lives in Asia and Africa is a carnivore with a specialized way of life that has evolved to fill a well-defined place, or ecological niche, in its environment. Each wild dog or fox not only interacts with its prey but also with all other predators in its surroundings, and, in this way, the balance of nature is maintained.

SOUTHERN SOLITAIRE
The Cape fox of South Africa is the most southern of the true foxes. It is a small solitary hunter (pp. 18–19) with a silvery coat. The Cape fox lives in dry places and hunts at dusk.

A MOST SOCIABLE DOG
The African hunting dog is one of the most social of all members of the dog family. It is not a dog (because it does not descend from the wolf), but belongs in a group – the genus *Lycaon* – on its own. These dogs live in large family packs on grasslands and have an elaborate system of communication, by means of body movements and sounds. Hunting by day, they range over a huge area in search of prey. They are vulnerable to disease and parasites, other hungry carnivores (such as lions), and being shot by humans.

Large, rounded ears

Short, broad face and muzzle

Thin, but well-muscled legs

Unique coat pattern is tan and grey with large white blotches

Having no dew claw on the front foot makes the hunting dog unique amongst the dog family

White tuft at the end of the short bushy tail acts as a flag

African hunting dog

Bat-eared fox

Very large ears, up to 12 cm (5 in) long

Dark grey to black on face mask and muzzle

Very long tail – up to 34 cm (13 in) in length

ENOUGH TEETH
The bat-eared fox (pp. 16–17) has 46 to 50 teeth – compared to 42 in other species of canid. It feeds mostly on insects but will also eat fruits.

TWO-HEADED FETISH
This medicine figure, or *Konde*, from Bakongo in Zaire, Africa, is used by driving nails into its wooden body to activate the forces within.

INDIAN OR CHINESE?
The red dog, or dhole, is a social hunter (pp. 18–19) with some characteristics like the African hunting dog, although apart from the rounded ears, they do not look at all alike. Neither of these canids will interbreed with domestic dogs. The Chinese dhole has a thicker, darker coat than the more southern Indian dhole.

Rounded ears

Dark red coat

Long, bushy tail

Chinese dhole

Tawny-coloured coat

Indian dhole

Tail darker colour than rest of coat

ON TOP OF THE WORLD
The Tibetan fox lives on the high, icy-cold plateaus of Tibet above 4,000 m (12,000 ft). It has a very thick furry coat to keep it warm and long slender jaws for pulling small rodents out of their burrows.

Tail is short, relative to its body length

White variety of coat shows this dog has been bred in captivity for its fur

Short, sharply pointed muzzle

Raccoon dog in winter coat

WHEN IS A RACCOON NOT A RACCOON?
The raccoon dog (above and right) has this name because it looks similar to a raccoon. It is a chubby canid with a short tail and a very thick, fine coat of grey-black and white fur. Because the coat is highly valued by the fur trade (pp. 12–13), the raccoon dog has been bred in captivity in many countries. In the USSR, captive animals were allowed to go wild and are now living as feral populations (pp. 36–37) which are spreading westwards.

Short, erect ears rounded at top

ONE LITTLE INDIAN
The Bengal fox is like a small red fox. It lives on open grasslands and scrub in India and digs its own dens. Like all foxes it hunts rodents, lizards, and other small animals.

Black facial mask, like that of a true raccoon

True raccoon of North and South America belongs to the Procyonidae family

Raccoon dog in dark summer coat

Red fox, grey fox

WAITING FOR LUNCH
Fox cubs (pp. 20–21) will stay with their mother for several months before they must leave her and find their own territories.

MAKING TRACKS
The paw prints of a fox are smaller than those of most dogs – the marks of the pads are longer, and the claws are sharply pointed.

Aʟʟ ꜰᴏxᴇꜱ ᴀʀᴇ ꜱᴏʟɪᴛᴀʀʏ ʜᴜɴᴛᴇʀꜱ that live on their own (pp. 18–19) – except in the mating season. They have long bodies, foxy faces, and a bushy tail, which is often called a "brush". Foxes have very highly developed senses (pp. 14–17), and large, erect ears. Their normal prey are rodents and rabbits, so they are useful at keeping down the numbers of these animals in the wild. The red fox is one of the most common carnivores in the world and is known to everyone from fables and stories for its cunning. Apart from the red fox there are ten other species in the fox group – or the genus *Vulpes* (pp. 26–27, 30–31). The grey fox of North and Central America belongs to another group – the genus *Urocyon*. It has different habits from the red fox and is noted for its ability to climb trees. The red fox is very adaptable and can live in many different environments from deserts and mountains to the centres of cities.

THE QUACK FROG
This is one of Greek storyteller, Aesop's (620–560 B.C.) many fables. It tells the story of a frog who claimed to be a learned doctor. The fox asked him why, if he was so skilled, did he not heal his own strange walk and wrinkled skin.

Coat can range in colour from greyish and rust-red to a flame red

FURRY BEAUTIFUL
The red fox's fur is so beautiful, that for thousands of years people have made clothes for themselves from their pelts. Captive foxes have also been bred for their furs in a variety of different coat colours. Today, clothes made of animal furs are unacceptable to many people who care about animals (pp. 12–13).

The tail of the red fox, which always has a white tip, does not express the animal's feelings the way the tail of a dog does

GETTING TO THE TOP

The grey tree fox is found in the United States (except in the Rocky Mountains and the northwest), Central America, and northern South America. It is a little smaller than the red fox, coloured grey like salt and pepper, and has reddish underparts, but the tail tip is never white.

A grey tree-climbing fox on the look-out for prey, which can be rabbits, insects, or dead animals (carrion)

Tip of the tail may be blackish, or grey like the coat

Nose and sides of muzzle are black

A BIRD IN VIEW

The red fox does not climb trees, where the grey fox spends much of its time in search of birds and eggs to kill and eat – from a scene printed on an English Wedgwood plate, c. 1764.

Fox's acute sense of smell enables it to cover distances of up to 10 km (6 miles) in search of food

Throat and chin have light, or white-coloured, fur

A HUNTING WE SHALL GO

In many countries fox hunting (pp. 14–15) is part of the sporting life of the countryside. Because they are such successful carnivores, foxes can become a pest to farmers by killing chickens and game birds. Hunting controls the numbers of foxes, but many people think it is cruel.

STREET WISE

In some cities foxes are becoming increasingly common. They kill rats, scavenge for food from dustbins, and even seem to learn road sense.

BLACK OR RED?

American artist John James Audubon (1785–1851) painted a wide variety of wildlife, including the black, or melanistic, form of the red fox.

DEEP IN THE FOREST

English artist William Morris (1834–1896), who designed this tapestry, had a great regard for the natural world. To him, as to many people today, the fox was an essential part of every woodland scene.

Hot foxes, cold foxes

N OT ALL SPECIES OF FOX have an easy life, living in the temperate parts of the world and hunting for rats, mice, and small birds. A few foxes live exceedingly harsh lives in the coldest – as well as in the hottest – lands. Only one fox lives in the icy cold Arctic regions of Alaska, Canada, northern Europe, and Asia, and that is the Arctic fox. These Arctic foxes have been known to cover a territory of 6,000 hectares (15,000 acres) in their search for food – they have short ears to cut down on heat loss and have dense fur to keep them warm in winter. There are also a number of different species of fox that live in the world's hottest deserts. Generally, very little food is available for the hot foxes, so they are adapted to be hunters and scavengers, ranging over huge areas in search of something to keep them alive. The foxes that live in hot, dry deserts all have very large ears which help to keep them cool, small bodies that can survive on little food, and short, dense fur. They sleep in dens, or hollows in the sand, during the intense heat of the day, and then hunt by night when it can actually be very cold.

DESERT FOX
The fennec fox is the smallest of all the foxes and it probably has the most difficult time of all in finding food. It lives in the parched deserts of Arabia and Africa's Sahara where there are very few other animals, so food is always scarce.

Soft, dense coat is designed to keep the Arctic fox warm, and is thicker in winter

Short, furry ears cut down on heat loss – in winter they must not become frostbitten

Dark brown and white summer coat

Adult's tail is very bushy, and can be as long as 30 cm (12 in)

Arctic fox cub in dark summer coat

COAT OF MANY COLOURS *above and right*
The Arctic fox can be seen in a coat of four different colours. The fox on the right is the white, or polar, form of its winter coat, and lives in the high Arctic where there is nearly always snow on the ground. In the summer, this fox will have a brown and white coat, as above. There is another less common variety of Arctic fox which is called "blue". The winter coat of the "blue" fox is steely-grey, but in summer it is brown all over. Moulting occurs twice a year – in spring and autumn – when it is time for a colour change.

A pair of Arctic foxes – one in a dark summer coat, the other in a pale winter coat

Hind foot has a thick covering of soft fur all over it – and under the pads

Big ears of the sand fox are typical of "hot foxes" – but not quite so big as those of the fennec

HALF A FENNEC FOX, HALF A RED FOX
Often confused with the fennec, this small desert fox from North Africa and the Arabian desert actually shares many characteristics with the red fox (pp. 28–29). Although its skull, teeth, and colouring are quite similar to the red fox's, this sand fox has a smaller body, is more delicately built, and has much bigger ears.

A WHITER SHADE OF PALE
The pale fox lives in grasslands at the southern edge of the Sahara desert in Africa. Like the fennec, it is a small, pale-coloured fox.

Long bushy tail can be curled around the body to keep it warm during cold desert nights

Rüppell's sand fox

Thick ruff of very fine fur around the neck

AFTER A MEAL
The fennec must have sharp senses (pp. 14–15) and quick movements if it is to catch these jumping rodents.

SWIFTLY, SWIFTLY
The kit, or swift, fox is the only desert fox in North America. Today, it is found only in the southwestern USA and Mexico. It used to be much more widespread until poisoned bait, put down for wolves and coyotes, also killed off many of these kit foxes.

The kit fox lives in the deserts of North America

Adult Arctic fox in pale winter coat

Thick fur on feet almost hides claws

South American mix

SOUTH AMERICAN WILD DOGS are often referred to as foxes, or "zorros" (the Spanish name for "foxes"), but they should not be confused with either true wolves (pp. 22–23), or true foxes (pp. 28–29). They are solitary hunters (pp. 18–19) of small animals, but they will also eat anything edible that they can find, including fruit. There are three distinct groups, or genera, of fox-like dogs: the short-legged bush dog; the maned wolf; and seven different members of the *Dusicyon* genus, of which the most common is the culpeo. The crab-eating zorro, also a member of the *Dusicyon* genus, is sometimes tamed by the Indians and will go hunting with them like a domestic dog. Another fox that used to live on the South American Falkland Islands, until the late 1800s, was exterminated by fur traders. Charles Darwin (1809–1882), English naturalist and author of *The Origin of the Species*, visited the Falklands in 1834 on his voyage around the world in the ship *HMS Beagle*, and described this animal as the "Falkland Island wolf".

CULPEO'S COAT
The culpeo's greyish-yellow and black coat, with a black-tipped tail, is not in demand for making fur clothing (pp. 12–13), so this canid is not, at present, in danger of extermination.

Stirrup vessel – with a fox on man's forehead – from Mochica tribe of pre-Columbian Peru, A.D. 300–1000

PRETTY PATAGONIAN
The Patagonian fox, or chilla, lives in the southern part of South America. Like many canids in the genus *Dusicyon*, it is not at all timid. In 1834, Darwin killed one by walking close and hitting it on the head with his geological hammer.

HEAVILY HUNTED
Found in the pampas of Argentina and southern Brazil, this grey-bodied, red-headed fox, or zorro, has a very long, bushy tail.

Azara's zorro

Small ears

Broad face

Bush dog

Reddish-tan, or tawny, coat

Very short legs

BUSH BADGER
The bush dog looks more like an otter, or badger, than a dog. Like other South American members of the dog family, this animal is not a true dog or fox, but belongs in a group – the genus *Speothos* – on its own. It is found in open country near water in tropical South America and spends much of its time in a burrow.

Large, erect ears with white fur inside

Erect mane with darker fur running down nape of neck and back

A DOG OF LITTLE EARS
The small-eared dog, or zorro, is one of the rarest of the South American dog family. It lives in the tropical rain forests but nothing is known of its habits.

Dark muzzle

MAGNIFICENT MANE

The maned wolf – in the genus *Chrysocyon* – is different from all other members of the dog family, in that its tail is very short and its legs are longer than the length of its body. This animal is not a wolf and it is not a fox, although it is sometimes called the "stilt-legged fox". The maned wolf lives in the tall grass and woodlands of southern Brazil, and hunts by pouncing on small animals.

Maned wolf

Very long, stilt-like legs

Reddish-yellow coat

Maned wolf's short, bushy tail has mostly white fur at its tip

Nazca pottery fox from coast of Peru, 500 B.C. – A.D. 600

THE CRAB-EATING ZORRO
This brindled-grey, crab-eating fox probably does not often eat crabs, so forest fox is a better name. It lives in the tropical forests of northeastern South America.

Dark-coloured fur on legs and feet make it look as if it is wearing stockings

Early domestication

Egyptian papyrus, c. 1500–1200 B.C., showing two jackals and some goats

THE WOLF IS THE ANCESTOR of all domestic dogs (pp. 48–61), including the Irish wolfhound, which is much larger than the wolf and the Pekingese, which is very much smaller. The outward shapes of these breeds may look completely different from the wolf and from each other, but inside its skin every dog feels and behaves like a wolf. Humans probably first began to live closely with tamed wolves during the last Ice Age, more than 12,000 years ago, and the bones of these early dogs are sometimes found on archaeological sites. The people of ancient Egypt and western Asia were the first to begin breeding distinctive kinds of dogs like mastiffs and greyhounds. By Roman times most of the different shapes and sizes of dogs, known today, were already in existence. This is known from the skeletal remains of these dogs, but more especially from models, paintings, and other works of art which often portray the animals in marvellous detail. In the ancient world, dogs were kept as hunting, herding, and guard dogs (pp. 40–45), for sport (pp. 46–47), and, as today, for companionship.

JACKAL GOD
The jackal has always had a close association with humans although it is not an ancestor of the domestic dog. Anubis, the jackal god, was a most important ancient Egyptian deity, and is here made of limestone, A.D. 300.

Handle decorated with coral

PERSIAN PLAQUE
This stylized half-dog, half-bird – or "fenmurv" – is a fertility symbol. Made of silver, c. 7th century A.D., sometime during the Sassanian dynasty, this object was found in northern India.

FRENCH FLAGON
This Celtic drinking vessel, made of bronze, c. 400 B.C., was found near Basse Yutz in France. Along the handle, two hounds chase a duck which seems to be swimming when liquid is poured.

ANCIENT HUNTSMEN
These Assyrian huntsmen, with their mastiff-like hounds, are walking in a royal park. This bas-relief is from Ashurbanipal's Palace at Nineveh, built between 645–635 B.C.

EASTERN WORSHIP

In the Far East, dogs are used for many purposes, and are included in religious worship. This stone temple god, in the form of a lion-like dog, is from Thailand.

GREEK URN

This beautiful vase is of Greek design (c. 380–360 B.C.), although it was found in southern Italy. The young girl is dangling a tortoise to tease her pet dog. The bracelets on her ankle are to ward off evil spirits.

The Townley hounds sculpture, collected by the Englishman Charles Townley (1737–1805), was found at Monte Cagnolo near Rome in Italy during the late 1700s

ONE WOMAN AND HER DOG

This is the skeleton of a woman who was buried with her hand resting on the body of her dog. The skeletons were found in Israel on an archaeological site called Ein Mallaha and are dated back to about 12,000 years ago. This is one of the earliest examples of a domestic dog ever to be discovered in the world.

TOWNLEY HOUNDS

The Romans kept dogs from the earliest times. They used greyhounds and bloodhounds for hunting, while large mastiffs were thought of as ideal, not only as fighting dogs, but also in war. This exquisite marble sculpture is of a pair of seated greyhounds from Rome, 2nd century A.D.

Italian brass collar

German spiked iron collar

DOGS' COLLARS

Ever since Egyptian times, dogs in paintings and sculpture have been shown wearing collars – from a painting in Pompeii, through a hunting scene in the Bayeux tapestries, to relatively modern times.

Silver presentation collar

CAVE CANEM

Just as today "Beware of the dog" is written on gates, the Romans wrote *Cave canem*, which means the same in Latin. This mosaic, c. 4th century A.D., comes from an entrance hall of a villa, excavated in Bodrum in Turkey.

DOG ROSE

The ancient Greeks thought this flower had magical qualities, and used it to treat people who had been bitten by a rabid (pp. 62–63) dog.

Pottery vessel – from the Colima culture in Mexico, A.D. 300–900 – of a hairless "techichi" dog, which was fattened for the table

Feral dogs

THE FIRST DOGS, DESCENDED from wolves, were domesticated about 12,000 years ago. Since then some domesticated dogs, like the dingo, have reverted to life in the wild and are known as "feral" dogs. They lived their own lives except when they could scavenge for a few scraps left by human hunters. In many parts of the world, dogs still live like this and they are not allowed too near to people. Quite often populations of dogs live and breed without any human contact at all. The most successful of all feral dogs is the dingo of Australia, but there are also feral dogs in India and many other parts of Asia, where they are called "pariah" dogs – "pariah" is a Tamil, or Sri Lankan, word meaning an "outcast". All over Africa feral dogs live on the outskirts of villages where they serve a useful function in cleaning up all the rubbish. At times these dogs are allowed into the houses but they are seldom given anything to eat because there is often not enough food for the people, let alone the animals. So the dogs must fend for themselves.

FERRETING FOR FOOD
The feral dogs of Egypt are sometimes lucky and find scraps of food left by tourists.

IN THE WILDS OF INDIA
Pariah dogs have been living wild in India for thousands of years. Some look very like the dingoes of Australia.

SANTO DOMINGO DOG
This dog must have looked very similar to the wild dogs that Christopher Columbus (1451–1506) probably found in the West Indies when he discovered America.

QUINKAN SPIRITS
In these cave paintings near Cape York in Australia, these "Quinkan spirits" – the Great Ancestors of the Aborigines – are accompanied by a dingo.

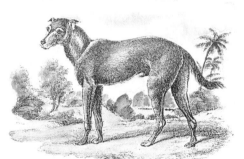

PERUVIAN PARIAH
Long before the Spanish first went to South America, the native peoples had dogs which lived around their settlements, just like their descendants – the feral dogs of today.

Nose is used for scenting prey – lizards, rabbits, or rodents, but sometimes fruit or plants

Eye of a dingo is more like that of a wolf, than a dog

A sitting dingo

THE AUSTRALIAN DOG
The dingoes of Australia (above and right) have been so successful at living in the wild that it has only recently been recognized that they were originally domestic dogs taken to Australia by the native Aborigines at least 4,000 years ago. Dingoes should be preserved as part of the unique animal kingdom of Australia because – except where they have interbred with European dogs – they are probably the only pure-bred descendants, left in the world, of prehistoric domestic dogs.

DOMINANT DINGO
These young dingoes know which one is the dominant dog.

THE ARISTOCRAT OF DOGS
The dingo, as depicted in this old engraving, is the aristocrat of all breeds. It is the most pure-bred dog in the world, because there are no other wild dogs with which to breed.

MOTHER AND BABIES
Like all dogs, the dingo is descended from the wolf (pp. 22–23). Like the wolf, the dingo mates once a year and brings up its young to be social hunters (pp. 18–19).

Coat is a tawny-yellow with pale underparts

Dingo's feet are like a wolf's – there is no dew claw on the hind foot

Tail is long and bushy – sometimes with a white tip

Feet are white in colour

Development of breeds

M ANY BREEDS OF DOG are hundreds of years old, like the spaniels, greyhounds, and terriers, but a new breed can be developed at any time by crossing two or more different breeds. The Sealyham terrier is one example of a new breed (pp. 52–53) that was developed in the 1800s by a Captain Edwardes who lived at Sealyham in Wales. It is also possible to reconstitute, or "remake", a breed that has become extinct. This was done with the Irish wolfhound which died out about a hundred years ago, but was bred as a new line from a cross of Great Danes, deerhounds, and mastiffs (pp. 48–49). Before the first dog show in England in 1859, there were considerable variations in the sizes, shapes, and colours of dogs within a single breed. Today, however, the dogs within one breed all look very similar, because of the required standards for showing. This can be harmful to the breeds as the dogs lose their individual characteristics. It can also lead to inherited ailments and is why German shepherd dogs are prone to dislocated hips.

Elegant lurcher shows typical bone structure of a dog

"YE OLDE MIMICKE DOGGE"
In the late 1500s there was an imaginary beast called a "Mimicke Dogge". Some people thought it probably had a shaggy coat and was good at performing tricks like a poodle, while others thought it had an "ape's wit and a hedgehog's face".

The turned-up corners of the mouth make this lurcher look as if it is smiling

IT'S RAINING CATS, DOGS, AND PITCHFORKS
This old English saying is not really true, but it may be based on ancient Chinese spirits for rain and wind, which were sometimes depicted as a cat and a dog. Here, the English caricaturist George Cruikshank (1792–1878) offers his interpretation.

Lurcher

SECRET SYMBOLS
American "kings of the road" – tramps, or hobos – used secret signs to let their friends know whether there was a dog (left), or a bad dog (below), on a stranger's property.

Dog

Bad dog

Wedgwood majolica (or highly glazed earthenware) punch-bowl, decorated with puppet Punch and his clown-dog Toby

BULL'S EYE
This bull terrier starred with Oliver Reed, who played Sikes in the 1968 film *Oliver!*, based on a novel by English writer Charles Dickens (1812–1870). Bull terriers were developed in the 1700s by crossing bulldogs and terrier-types to produce a fierce fighting dog (pp. 46–47). Their small, fine, erect ears were developed to avoid illegal ear-cropping (pp. 44–45).

A FIGHT TO THE FINISH
The Staffordshire bull terrier first entered the show ring as a recognized breed in 1935. It was developed in the Midlands of England, originally as a fighting dog, by crossing the old-fashioned bull terrier with the bulldog and the now extinct Old English terrier.

Very muscular body

Small, half-pricked ears

Staffordshire bull terrier

V-shaped ears, falling forwards

Dark, deep-set eyes

THE ROUGH AND THE SMOOTH
These popular terriers were first bred in the 1800s by Jack Russell, a clergyman from Devon, England. These small dogs were produced by several, now extinct breeds and varied much in appearance and size. Once considered by Kennel Clubs to be a type, not a breed, the British Kennel Club made the Parson Jack Russell – but not all Jack Russells – an official breed in 1990. The Australian Jack Russell is recognized as a breed there, but in Canada and the USA Jack Russells are considered types, not breeds.

Coat can be long and rough-haired, or short and smooth-haired

Jack Russell terriers

Streamlined body and short-haired coat make a dog built for speed

Thomas Bewick's (pp. 42–43) engraving of an old-fashioned lurcher

IN THE LURCH
Originally a cross-breed (pp. 60–61) between a greyhound and a terrier, its patience and intelligence, speed and fighting ability, made it a perfect dog for a poacher (pp. 40–41). A "type" of dog, rather than a "breed", the lurcher may be well on its way to becoming a recognized breed, as many owners would like to enter their dogs in the show ring.

HEAD OVER HEELS
It's hard to say what breed this little dog is – but he's certainly surprised his mistress with his amusing antics.

Hunting dogs

HUNTING IN INDIA
The Mughal emperors of India had just as many rituals of hunting as the feudal lords of medieval Europe. Akbar (1542–1605) is shown here hunting blackbuck, or Indian antelope, with Saluki-type hounds.

DOGS WERE USED IN HUNTING wild animals all over the world for centuries. In medieval times, hunting from horseback with dogs became an important part of life for the kings and feudal lords of Europe. Hunting was considered necessary as training for tournaments of chivalry and for warfare. The laws of hunting, or venery as it then was called, were very complicated, with the result that certain animals were preserved for only the nobility to hunt.
Important "beasts of venery" were the red deer stag (male) and hind (female), the hare, wild boar, and wolf, while the fallow deer, roe deer, fox, and wild cat were considered of secondary value and were called "beasts of the chase". Special breeds of scent and sight hounds (pp. 14–17) were used at different times during these hunts and were kept in royal kennels. The most valuable dogs were buckhounds.

MEDIEVAL HUNTING DOGS
Medieval huntsmen usually had a pack of at least 12 running hounds and a well-trained scent hound, or lyme-hound, whose task was to frighten the game out of its hiding place. In this detail of a picture in *Benninck's Book of Hours*, it is a wild boar.

COME BLOW THE HORN
Blowing the horn with a series of long and short notes was a very important part of the rituals of medieval hunting.

The Savernake Horn was made of ivory in 12th-century England. Scenes of hunting, engraved in silver, were added in the 14th century

THE THRILL OF THE CHASE
A horse, rider, and hunting dogs chase a stag along this French watchchain, beautifully crafted in silver and gold in 1845.

GAMEKEEPER AND HIS DOGS
Many traditions connected with hunting and shooting remain unchanged since medieval times. The gamekeeper's job of protecting game from predators and poachers is still the same as it was when the laws of venery were first enacted in the 11th century.

BENIN PIECE
The Benin bronzes from Nigeria are famous throughout the world for their great artistic value. This bronze plaque, made by a Nigerian artist in the late 16th century, is of a Portuguese soldier with his gun and hunting dog.

RUNNING WITH THE PACK
This late 19th-century painting, by British artist Alfred Duke (died 1905), shows a pack of hunting beagles picking up the scent and creating a noisy clamour. These bold, strong, intelligent dogs may have an ancient origin. The Norman French used them for pursuing hares – they were so small that they were carried in the saddlebags or pockets of mounted hunters.

SWIMMING DOG
This golden retriever has been told to fetch a stick out of the water, but it would collect a dead animal killed in a hunt just as quickly. Most dogs enjoy a swim, but retrievers are specially bred to bring back birds and other animals that have been shot and have fallen into the water. These dogs are trained to respond quickly to commands. They have "a soft mouth" which means they can carry a dead bird in their mouths without biting into it. Their fur has a very thick, water-resistant undercoat.

DIANA THE HUNTRESS
This painting in enamel on a metal plaque from Limoges shows what hunting hounds looked like in France in the mid 16th century. The picture is of Diana, the Roman goddess of the hunt. There are many legends about Diana who shunned the society of men and was attended always by a large number of nymphs. In classical art she was often shown in a chariot drawn by two white stags.

All dogs swim by paddling with their front legs, just like children do when they are learning to swim by "doggy-paddling"

Herding and sheepdogs

THE USE OF DOGS TO PROTECT and herd livestock dates from as early as 1000 B.C. when farmers began to breed large numbers of sheep, goats, and cattle. In his book on looking after farm animals, in the first century A.D., the Roman writer, Columella, noted that shepherds preferred white sheepdogs because they could be distinguished from wolves. There was always a danger that the shepherd would kill his own dog, believing it to be a wolf that was about to kill his animals. Even today, although the wolf is nearly extinct, most of the great variety of herding dogs that are bred in nearly every country of the world, are still tan or light-coloured with a lot of white in their coats.

ROUGH COLLIE
The original rough collie was the traditional sheepdog of the lowlands of Scotland, and probably took its name from a "colley", or local black sheep. For hundreds of years it was an essential partner for every shepherd. Today, the rough collie is one of the world's most popular breeds and has become a most successful show dog and companion everywhere.

Straight, muscular forelegs and powerful, sinewy hindlegs enabled the rough collie to cover great distances while herding sheep

OLD DOG'S TAIL
Old English sheepdogs are seldom born without tails, and most puppies have their tails docked (pp. 44–45) for showing. A heavy sheepdog without a tail is not much use because it cannot run fast. Although called "Old", this breed is probably not of ancient origin. In this 19th-century English painting, the sheepdog is ready to tend its sheep.

Long-haired, thick coat is usually pale gold, tan, and white, with dark hair around the head

BELGIAN SHEPHERD DOG
There were no wolves left in Belgium when the shepherd dogs of this country were first developed as distinct breeds in the 1880s. Therefore they, and indeed the modern German shepherd dog, are an exception to the tradition that herding dogs should be light-coloured.

ROUND-UP TIME
The Border collie, originally from the border country between England and Scotland, is one of the finest sheepdogs in the world. It is bred as a working dog, not for showing.

THE BLUE HEELER
The Australian cattle dog is now the official name for this breed of strong working dog, developed by cattlemen in the 1830s. It has had a number of previous names, such as the Queensland blue heeler. These dogs round up cattle by nipping at their heels.

A SHEPHERD AND HIS DOG
This Romanian shepherd and his dog are
both well-prepared for the rigours of the
winters in central Europe. These traditional
breeds – of both sheepdog and shepherd –
are heavily built, have thick coats,
and are excellent guardians
of the flock.

IMPASSE
Englishman Thomas Bewick (1753–1828) was
famous for his animal engravings. Here
a dog teases
a bull.

*The ears should be
semi-erect with the
tips pointing
forwards*

SMALL BUT BEAUTIFUL
All the domestic animals
on the Shetland Isles, off the
north coast of Scotland, tend to
be very small. Small animals,
like the Shetland pony
and Shetland cattle,
thrive best in the
tough conditions – the
climate is very cold and
windy, and food is often
scarce, especially in winter.
The Shetland sheepdog,
or sheltie, is also a
successful product of
breeding for small
size. A tiny version
of the Scottish
rough collie, it
was the traditional
herding dog of the
Shetland Isles.

*The sheltie's good
sense of smell can
seek out and save
a lamb that is
buried in the
snow*

Helper dogs

To catch a thief

DOGS HAVE BEEN INDISPENSABLE throughout history as helpers in human societies. Besides being used to herd other animals and for companionship, their principal function has been as guardians of the home and farm. Today the job of the guard dog has been extended to protection of factories and industrial estates. To shut up a dog on its own in an empty building or other enclosed space and expect it to live by itself, and to ward off intruders, goes against all the social behavioural patterns of the dog, and is cruel. Dogs that are trained by the police for protection and for detection of drugs and explosives are seldom alone and normally live well-balanced lives. Certain breeds are more innately aggressive than others, but nearly all dogs have to be specially trained to be aggressive to strangers and not to their handlers. Today there are innumerable other ways in which dogs help the sick, the disabled, and the lonely, and by insisting on a daily walk they keep their owners healthy.

DOGS OF WAR
The intense loyalty of dogs to people means that they can be trained to carry out missions under conditions of great danger.

Strong teeth and a sturdy jaw – with the lower jaw projecting above the upper – help the boxer to keep strangers at bay

Boxers have great strength and energy – the powerful forequarters are inherited from the bulldog

Thick black and tan coat is long and wavy and provides perfect protection against the intense cold of the Swiss mountains

BERNESE MOUNTAIN DOG
In the old days the large mastiff-type dogs in Switzerland were used for protecting merchants, cattle traders, drovers, and their herds as they travelled through the mountain passes. Until the early 1900s they were all known simply as Swiss mountain dogs, but today there are four separate breeds – the Bernese (pp. 56–57) from the province, or canton, of Berne; the Appenzell from the canton of the same name; the Entelbuch from the canton of Lucerne; and the Greater Swiss.

St Bernard to the rescue

RESCUE DOGS
For several hundred years, dogs bred at the monastery of the Great Saint Bernard Pass in Switzerland were trained to rescue travellers lost in the mountains.

A DOG WITH THREE HEADS
In ancient mythology, Cerberus was a three-headed dog that stood at the gates of hell – to prevent the living from entering and the dead from leaving.

DOGS IN SPACE
Sending dogs into space may have contributed greatly to human knowledge, but for the dogs it must have been a terrifying experience – no different from any other laboratory experiment. The first dog to be sent into space was the Russian dog Laika in 1957.

БЕЛКА И СТРЕЛКА

German shepherd dogs have plenty of room in their straight, wolf-like jaws for strong, healthy teeth

Cutting the ears to make them permanently erect (cropping) is illegal in Britain, but it is done in other countries to make the dog look fiercer

SEEING EYE DOGS
Everyone knows how dogs can be trained to be "the eyes" of people who are blind. They can also learn to help the deaf, and disabled people who need a helping hand to pick up objects, as well as providing companionship to the old, the sick, and the deprived.

Cutting off the tail (docking) is a cruel mutilation that prevents the dog from expressing its natural behaviour

This Dobermann is warning an intruder to come no closer

THE FIERCE DOBERMANN
The Dobermann is a born guard dog, and has been bred to be aggressive. But like nearly all dogs, when correctly reared, it can also be an affectionate companion. The breed was first developed in Germany at the end of the 19th century.

GOOD COMPANIONS
The boxer and the German shepherd dog (pp. 10–11) are both guard dogs and were first bred in Germany. The boxer is of mastiff origin (pp. 34–35) crossed with the bulldog (pp. 54–55), and the German shepherd dog is a droving, or herding, dog that has become the most popular guardian and protector of property world-wide. Dogs of both breeds will also be loyal and affectionate companions for people if reared and trained correctly, but they need plenty of space and exercise.

The powerful hindquarters make the German shepherd dog a good jumper and able to cover great distances without getting tired

BRAVE GUARD DOG
As long as this dog can spend most of the time with a person, it will be content and can be trained to protect and guard people and buildings.

45

Dogs in sport

DOGS HAVE BEEN USED, over the ages, in a great variety of sports, many of which have been regrettably associated with much cruelty. In Roman times the sport of baiting animals, such as bears and bulls (pp. 54–55), became very fashionable and continued until the late 1800s. Today, most people find it inconceivable that anyone should want to watch a dog-fight, or a badger being baited and torn to death by a group of dogs. But, although illegal, these activities are still practised in some parts of Britain. However, dogs like to compete with each other and there are many sports which are not so cruel. The large number of different breeds of sight hound (pp. 14–15) have all been developed for coursing, or chasing after, fast-running prey such as hares. They were often used – together with birds of prey – in the sport of falconry. In northern Africa and Asia, both the Saluki and the Afghan hound (pp. 48–49) were bred for chasing gazelles. Today, in greyhound racing, dogs are bred for speed, and run after a mechanical "hare".

GOING TO THE DOGS
Greyhounds, together with whippets, are the number one choice for dog racing in stadiums around the world. Here, though, the greyhound is used for advertising Camembert cheese.

"THE DOG FIGHT"
The spectators in this painting, by English artist Thomas Rowlandson (1756–1827), are urging on their dogs to fight and are betting on which dog will win. Today this cruel sport is illegal in Britain and many other countries.

Keen sight of the borzoi (pp. 14–15) will help it to win a race – or, as in former times, to hunt well

MUZZLED
Dogs get very excited when they are racing, so usually they wear muzzles to stop them biting other dogs during a race.

Borzoi

Deep chest and freely swinging shoulders enable the dog to take long strides

Long, muscular lower legs

*Well-feathered tail is long,
set low, and gently curved*

Well-muscled legs make the Saluki a powerful runner

THE ROYAL SALUKI
The Saluki is one of the oldest breeds of sight hound (pp. 14–15) in the world and dogs of this type can be seen in the tomb paintings of ancient Egyptian Pharaohs. For thousands of years Salukis have been bred by Arab peoples for chasing gazelle and, together with falcons, for killing large birds, such as bustards.

AWAY TO THE RACES
Although dogs have been used in the Arctic for hundreds of years to draw sleds (pp. 56–57), today they have been mostly replaced by mechanical snowmobiles. However, within recent years, the sport of sled-racing over long distances with huskies has become very popular – especially in Alaska, the northernmost state in the USA.

TINTIN AND SNOWY
These popular cartoon characters race over the snow with their trusty team of huskies.

Dense, curly ruff on neck

*Long, wavy, silky
hair is usually
white with attractive
dark markings*

*Ankle joint, or
hock, is high up
which makes the
leg very long
and powerful*

THE HARE AND THE DOG
The use of greyhounds for hare-coursing – pursuing game with dogs that follow by sight, not scent – is probably one of the most ancient of all sports.

BEAUTIFUL BOUNDER
The borzoi comes from Russia and used to be called the Russian wolfhound because it was used by the aristocracy for hunting and chasing wolves. The borzoi may have been developed from long-legged, southern, sight hounds (pp. 14–15), like the Saluki, which were then crossed with long-haired, local, collie-type dogs. They were bred to look as aristocratic and beautiful as possible to match the noble aspirations of the Russian emperors.

Hounds

THE HOUND GROUP OF DOGS was one of the most distinctive, after the various dogs were separated into their different groups. Hound-like dogs featured on many historical objects. At a later stage, hounds became divided into sight hounds, like the greyhound and the Afghan hound, and scent hounds, like the bloodhound. Sight hounds (pp. 14–15) were lightly built, very fast running, and were used in the hunt to chase prey. Scent hounds (pp. 16–17) were more heavily built, slower in action, and were used to scent out prey and put it up for the chase. Hounds vary in size more than any other dog group. The Irish wolfhound, originally a sight hound used for hunting wolves, is the heaviest of all dogs, while the dachshund, a scent hound used for hunting badgers, is one of the smallest. Many breeds of hound are still used today for hunting but others, such as the wolfhound, are house dogs and companions. The lifespan of small hounds is around 15 years, but very large hounds live on average for only about half this time.

ELEGANT BORZOI
The borzoi (pp. 14–15) is the most aristocratic of all hounds, and it looks as though it would hardly deign to behave like an ordinary dog.

WELSH LEGEND
The town of Beddgelert in Wales is named after the famous deerhound Gelert, killed by Prince Llewellyn, after he thought the dog had killed his child. The Prince found blood all around the baby's cradle so he killed the dog with his sword. But then he found the baby safe, and nearby a dead wolf, killed by his faithful dog. This Welsh legend is one of several similar stories known in many countries around the world.

Wrinkled brow and face

Long, silky ears

"Dewlap" or loose folds of skin hanging beneath the throat

Short hair on face and along the back

LONG-HAIRED BEAUTY
The Afghan hound is an ancient breed of long-haired greyhound that originated in Afghanistan, where it was used by the royal family for hunting gazelle, or small antelope. When it was first shown in Britain, the Afghan's long, silky coat caused a sensation. The Afghan hound is a popular show dog but retains its hunting and racing instincts.

Very long, silky hair

TALLYHO
The foxhound has changed little since medieval times and it is still used today for fox hunting. Foxhounds do not make good house dogs because, for centuries, they have been bred only for hunting, and for living in large numbers close together as a pack.

A DIGNIFIED DOG
In modern times the role of the bloodhound has been as a guard dog rather than a hunting hound, but its fearsome reputation as a relentless tracker has survived in legend if not in fact. Breeding for show standards has led to the folds of skin around its head becoming over-developed and extreme, and this can lead to health problems.

THE HOUND OF THE BASKERVILLES
Shown above is a still from one of three film versions of British writer Sir Arthur Conan Doyle's (1859–1930) most famous Sherlock Holmes story.

THE GREAT DOG OF IRELAND
The ancient breed of hounds used in Ireland since medieval times for hunting wolves probably died out completely in the 19th century – more than 100 years after the last wolf was killed in Ireland. A British army officer recreated the breed in the late 1800s and since then the Irish wolfhound has become a giant. It is the tallest dog in the world, with a shoulder height of up to 94 cm (3 ft). However, the old Irish wolfhound looked more like a rough-haired greyhound.

Tail is carried erect, not curled forwards

HUNTING HARE
The beagle was originally bred for tracking hares in Britain and France, but it is now very popular in North America where it is used for hunting cottontail rabbits. Because they are small, have a uniform weight, and tolerate living together in large numbers, beagles have become the breed most frequently used for laboratory research.

A DEVONSHIRE HUNTING TAPESTRY
This detail, from one of four Flemish tapestries woven in the early 1400s, shows a medieval hunting scene with richly dressed ladies and noblemen, their hounds, and prey of boar. These tapestries were once owned by the Duke of Devonshire in England.

Straight, strong forelegs and long, muscular hindlegs enabled the Irish wolfhound to cover great distances in chasing its prey

SOMETIMES A "SAUSAGE" DOG
Dachshund means "badger-dog" in German and the breed was originally an "earth dog" – a terrier used to dig out badgers from their dens. Because "hund" was translated into English as "hound", these dogs became classed in that group. The miniature dachshund is a popular house dog, weighing up to 5 kg (11 lb).

The dachshund can have three varieties of coat – short-haired, long-haired, or, as here, wire-haired

Gun dogs

SPANIELS, SETTERS, pointers, and retrievers all fall within the category of dogs called "gun dogs" in Britain and "sporting dogs" in North America. The breeds are not usually aggressive, having been originally bred to live together in kennels. Gun dogs are today mostly used for shooting game birds. They are trained to "point" and "set" (pp. 16–17). They must scent the air for the birds and then stay still and silent in a crouching position, to make the presence of the birds known to the hunters, without chasing them. Gun dogs must also have soft mouths so that they can retrieve the dead or wounded prey undamaged by their teeth (pp. 40–41). Gun dogs respond very well to training – for this reason they are bred not only for sport but also as house dogs and companions. The Labrador retriever is probably the most popular animal companion and helper dog (pp. 44–45) worldwide.

READY, AIM, FIRE
Above all else, the huntsman's dog must not be afraid of the noise of a gun.

English setter holds a stick in its mouth, in the same way as it would a bird

An object for training a gun dog to become used to holding prey in its mouth

English setter's thick coat enables it to be used for hunting in winter and to endure the cold weather

AT THE END OF THE DAY
Along with their hunting dogs (pp. 40–41) and a horse, these huntsmen, wearing hacking jackets and riding breeches and holding their guns, are at rest after a long day's hunt.

BRINGING HOME A BIRD
The retriever is trained to bring back to the huntsman, or retrieve, game after it has been shot.

Setters and pointers often hold up one front foot as they "freeze" into position before the shoot

RED-HAIRED BEAUTY
The Irish, or red, setter has a very silky coat and a gentle nature. However, the red setter is a highly strung and headstrong breed, and it is often considered to be unreliable as a gun dog.

A REAL CHARMER
Now a show dog and pet, but bred as a gun dog, the American cocker spaniel got its name from its ability to flush out the birds called woodcock.

Muscular, strong-boned legs helped the cocker to be an excellent bird dog

A DAMP DAY FOR DUCK HUNTING
Duck shooting often ends up with both the huntsman and his dog getting very wet. Spaniels, which have been bred for hundreds of years as water dogs, are the traditional companions of the wildfowler. In this painting are a Chesapeake retriever, a curly-coated retriever, and an Irish water spaniel (from left to right).

GETTING THE POINT
Pointers are trained to "point" (pp. 16–17) at hidden game with their noses. This makes them essential companions on bird shoots.

Dog made of Italian glass decorates lid of Austrian box, c. 1800

Tail is called "feathered" when it looks like the feathers of a bird

GOOD SHOT
This 18th-century tile from France shows a huntsman – wearing a shoulder pouch for collecting the game – and his gun dogs chasing the prey which is probably a rabbit, or a hare.

SETTING UP THE GAME
The English setter is one of the oldest and perhaps the most beautiful breeds of gun dog. Originally, the setter was a spaniel that was trained to "set" the game – to put the birds up so that they could be killed. In the Middle Ages the birds were caught in nets but later on they were shot with guns.

Special long lead allows gun dogs to escape their leash quickly

Terriers

TARTAN TERRIER
The modern Scottish terrier, or "Scottie", is descended from short-legged, rough-coated, working terriers that were bred for centuries in the Scottish Highlands. Generally, the Scottie was not black until the 1900s.

TERRIERS ARE "EARTH DOGS"– *terra* means "the earth" in Latin. They are great diggers and they need no encouragement to go down holes in the ground in pursuit of badgers, foxes, rabbits, or rats. Terriers have an ancient history in Britain and have always been used as small sporting and hunting dogs. They are the best dogs for killing rats on farms and down mines. Traditionally, different types of terrier have been bred in many regions of Britain – like the Border, Scottish, and Yorkshire terriers – but a few other countries have also developed new breeds, such as the Australian terrier. Many of the terriers registered by the Kennel Clubs of today have only been distinguished as separate breeds in the last hundred years.

The tip of the Airedale's small, V-shaped ear falls forwards to the top of its eye

Strong teeth and vice-like jaws prevent prey escaping

Coat is stiff, wiry, and lies close to the body, thereby requiring careful grooming (pp. 62–63)

Long, strong jaws help the Australian terrier catch rabbits, rats, and even snakes

A SHAGGY DOG STORY
Early British immigrants to Australia took their dogs with them, and by the early 1900s, this new breed – the Australian terrier – had been developed, from a mix of Cairn, Dandie Dinmont, Irish, Scottish, and Yorkshire terriers.

A ROMAN DOG
Discovered in northern England during the 1800s, this copper alloy figure (made between the first and fourth centuries A.D.) looks rather like an old terrier breed – the Aberdeen.

The ears of the low-slung, compact Norfolk terrier are slightly rounded at the tip and drop forwards close to its cheek

Given a rubber ring, or ball, the playful nature of a terrier is quite apparent

A GIANT AMONG TERRIERS

The Airedale terrier is named after the district in Yorkshire, England where it originated. The largest of all terriers, it was developed in the mid 1800s by cross-breeding (pp. 60–61) the now extinct black-and-tan terrier with the otterhound to increase its size and strength for the hunting of large prey. It was also used in World War I as a messenger dog (pp. 44–45).

Tail is set well up, and carried erect, not curved forwards over its back

A LEGEND IN HIS OWN LIFETIME

When "Greyfriars" died in Edinburgh, Scotland, this little Skye-type terrier – the ever-faithful "Bobby" – refused to leave his master's grave until he himself died, ten years later – or so the story goes.

FOXY FELLOW

In the late 1800s, the fox terrier was the most popular breed of dog in England. Today this popularity has been overtaken by the smaller Jack Russell terrier (pp. 38–39). Fox terriers can be either wire-haired like this one, or smooth-haired.

With excellent balance, a wire-haired fox terrier is ready for action – whether tearing up a carpet or hunting foxes (pp. 28–29)

DECORATED "DRUMMER" DOG

Dogs have always been popular as mascots, usually with army regiments, as shown here. This brave war hero is "Drummer", the Northumberland Fusiliers' mascot whose death was reported in a British newspaper in 1902.

Bedlington's long ears, pear-shaped head, and curly, light-coloured coat make it look more like a lamb

LIKE A LAMB

All sorts of breeds, including the whippet, otterhound, and bull terrier are thought to have contributed to the development of the Bedlington terrier, at one time known as the Rothbury terrier.

DANDIFIED DOG

Dogs have been used in advertising for a long time. A terrier in his finery here graces a magazine cover.

DIGGER BONES

The Norfolk terrier is a new breed that is descended from terriers bred in East Anglia, England for hundreds of years. It is a very sporting little dog with short legs and a wiry coat. The Norwich terrier had both prick-, and drop-eared, varieties, but in 1965 the name of Norfolk was given to those with drop ears.

Terriers – like this Norfolk – dig with both their front and hind legs

Utility dogs

T HE WORD "UTILITY" MEANS USEFULNESS, and as most dogs are useful to humans in one way or another, the American name of "Non-sporting dogs" is more appropriate than "Utility dogs" for this mixed group of breeds. This miscellaneous collection of dogs includes the ones left over after all the other breeds have been neatly slotted into the other five groups (pp. 48–53, 56–59). However, the title of "Special dogs" might be more apt in order to cover the range of their individual, and special, characteristics – they certainly include the more interesting, unusual dogs. Their history, in some cases, goes back for many centuries – the forerunner of the chow chow was first bred in Mongolia, in Asia, 3,000 years ago for use in war, and later, in China, as a source of fur and food. In fact, most of the dogs in this group have been bred for some particular purpose in the past, like the bulldog for bull-baiting, and the poodle for hunting water fowl, but today they live only as companions and show dogs. This group also includes national dogs from various countries – the Boston terrier from the USA, the bulldog from Britain, and the poodle from France.

MADE IN AMERICA
The Boston terrier is a very popular dog in the USA and is one of the few breeds to have been developed there.

USEFUL HELPERS
In this detail from a 17th-century Japanese screen, a richly dressed Portuguese merchant is shown with his servants, and faithful companion – his dog.

The back has retained the powerful muscles of the old-fashioned bulldog

Legs are set wide apart allowing the dog to stand its ground

French bulldog

BAT-EARED BULLDOG
In the old days French bulldogs were used for baiting donkeys – setting on an animal for sport (pp. 46–47). Today they are smaller and live more peaceful lives, but it is still a tough breed and a good guard dog.

The tongue of the chow chow is always blue-black, an unusual characteristic inherited from the dog's Chinese ancestors

CHINESE CHOW
The breed of chow chow is now 200 years old, having been developed from a pair of dogs of pariah origin (pp. 36–37) introduced into England from Canton in southeast China in the 1780s. English naturalist Gilbert White (1720–1793) in his *The Natural History of Selborne* (1789) described the dogs as "such as are fattened in that country for the purpose of being eaten".

Very thick fur and curled tails are typical of spitz dogs, like the chow chow, for adapting to sub-Arctic temperatures

THE BEST OF BRITISH
The bulldog is the national symbol of the British, portraying strength and stubbornness. This breed was developed for bull-baiting – setting dogs to attack bulls for public sport – and dates back to at least the 16th century.

JUMPING THROUGH HOOPS
Because the poodle is one of the most easily trained of breeds, it has been commonly used as a circus dog. In this fine gold brooch, made in Austria, c. 1890, a clown encourages his troop of dogs to perform tricks.

THE ELEGANT "COACH-DOG"
In the 1800s, it was very fashionable in England and France to have a "coach-dog" to accompany the carriages of aristocrats. The horses' harness and dog's coat colours could be colour coordinated.

Muzzle is adorned by a massive moustache

This strongest of all the schnauzers – the giant schnauzer – stands up to 65 cm (2 ft) at the shoulder

BUSHY-HAIRED BEAUTY
Schnauzers got their name from the German word *Schnauze* meaning "muzzle". Originally used for herding sheep in southern Germany, nowadays these energetic dogs make excellent companions and family pets. In the USA and Canada the giant and standard schnauzers are classified as "working dogs" (pp. 56–57), while the miniature is in the "terrier group" (pp. 52–53).

The Dalmatian's coat is always pure white with distinctive black or brown (liver) spots

SPOTTED DOG
There are several legends about the origin of the Dalmatian. Some people believe that the dogs came from India with gypsies who settled in Dalmatia, in western Croatia; others think that the breed originated in Italy. Dalmatians were first brought to England by travellers to Europe in the 18th century. It then became fashionable to have aristocratic-looking dogs running beside the carriage horses of gentlemen. The Dalmatian is unique in that it excretes urea, and not uric acid, in its urine. This means that it should be a popular breed with gardeners because its urine does not kill lawn grass.

Legs are long and built for speed and endurance

PRETTY AS A PICTURE
Poodles were first bred as gun dogs (pp. 50–51), probably in Germany, but their intelligence and attractive appearance soon led to their chief role of much-loved house dog. An early form of the pet poodle as it was in the 1700s is shown in this painting by Jean Jacques Bachelier (1724–1806).

Working dogs

SUPERIOR SWIMMER
The huge Newfoundland breed may originate from Pyrenean mountain rescue dogs taken to Newfoundland in eastern Canada by Spanish fishermen.

ROYAL CORGI
Short-legged cattle dogs, called corgis, have lived in Wales since medieval times. They are now the favourites of British royalty.

THE EARLIEST DOMESTIC DOGS, which were descended from tamed wolves about 12,000 years ago (pp. 34–35), were companions to human hunters in their pursuit of all sorts of animals from mammoths to small birds. Over the thousands of years since that time, dogs have always worked with people. Before Europeans reached North America in the 15th century A.D., the dog was the only animal that had been domesticated by the American Indians. The chief work of these dogs was to draw a sled, or "travois", laden with possessions, when a family moved from place to place. They were also used to help in the great hunts of bison when a whole herd could be driven to its death. In Europe, where there have been horses and oxen for drawing carts, dogs have not been so commonly used for draught work, although Eskimo dogs and huskies have been indispensable in polar exploration. For the purposes of dog shows, the breed registry includes herding dogs (pp. 42–43), as well as helper dogs (pp. 44–45) in the category of working dogs.

AGILE AUSSIE
The job of the Australian kelpie is to round up sheep that have strayed from the main flock – it has the odd ability of running along sheep's backs to reach the head of the flock. A well-trained dog can do the work of six men and it is able to travel 64 km (40 miles) in a day.

Colour of a husky's eyes can be brown or blue – or even one of each

Siberian husky

Dogs lose heat through their tongues, which is why they pant to cool down – even in the Arctic

Thick ruff of fur around neck, and stocky shape keep as much warmth inside the husky's body as possible

SWISS BLANKET
The Bernese mountain dog, a typical helper dog (pp. 44–45), is an example of many breeds of mastiff-type dogs that have been used throughout Europe and Asia since the Roman period, for guarding and protecting travellers in the mountains. By sleeping beside the traveller at night, the dog's exceptionally thick fur would keep both human and animal warm, and by day the dog would be able to follow the path with its nose, even through thick snow.

SPECIAL DELIVERY
In Switzerland and other very mountainous countries, mastiff-type dogs were the best animals for drawing milk carts steadily along narrow paths. From earliest times (pp. 34–35) its natural aggression made the mastiff an excellent guard dog.

The Great Dane,
like all mastiffs,
has a very deep
and powerful chest

IN THE GREAT FAR NORTH
The word "Eskimo" means "snow".
It is no longer used for the Inuit and
other native North Americans who
live in the Arctic regions, but the
name has remained in use
for their dogs.

WHEN IS A DANE NOT A DANE?
The Great Dane was developed in Germany,
where in the old days no castle was complete
without a pair of these giant mastiff-type dogs
to guard it.

The working dog's
harness is designed to
give it the greatest
pulling power

The tail trails
when the dog is
working or at
rest, but curves
over its back
when running

HARNESSING A HUSKY
The Siberian husky and the
Alaskan malamute are the only
pure breeds of husky. Otherwise,
the name is used in North America,
particularly Canada, for all the dogs
of the spitz type that are used for
drawing sleds and for hunting seals
and other Arctic animals. Peoples who
have lived for thousands of years in the
Arctic zones of North America,
Europe, and Asia could not have
survived without their
working huskies and
Eskimo dogs (pp. 46–47).

HERALDIC DOG
Images of dogs have often
appeared in heraldry. This
husky is an important part
of the coat of arms for
Canada's Yukon Territory.

Toy dogs

Dismal Desmond – a popular stuffed toy from 1930s' England – lives up to his name

THE CATEGORY OF TOY DOGS INCLUDES all the smallest show breeds, with most dogs having a height of less than 30.5 cm (12 in). Perhaps one of the most remarkable facts of all about the domestication of animals is that every single toy dog, however small, is descended from the wolf. Because, genetically, it has inherited the same characteristics as its wild ancestor, even the tiniest dog will try its best to behave like a wolf. It will gnaw at bones, it will guard its territory, and it will show its feelings to other dogs with its posture and tail – just like a wolf does. The Romans were probably the first to breed miniature dogs, and bones have been found on Roman excavations of dogs that are as small as any of today's breeds. The small white dogs known as Maltese (pp. 10–11) are probably of Roman origin, and a dog of this type can be seen in a Roman painting. Other tiny dogs have been bred since ancient times in Tibet, China, and Japan, while in Europe, toy spaniels were the favourite companions of the aristocracy throughout the Middle Ages.

Small, V-shaped ears set high on head

Fine, silky-textured coat is long except on face and ears

DOG'S DINNER
In a detail from this charming, 19th-century, French painting, entitled *Caninemania*, the family pet is treated as a very special dinner guest – to the exclusion of the lady's friend who has been relegated to a seat in the corner – and is, therefore, out of the picture.

Large, broad head with very flat profile and a snub nose

TOY TERRIER TERROR
The Australian silky terrier is not a toy by nature. This short-legged, compact dog can kill a rat or a rabbit in seconds, and it is claimed to be equally quick at killing snakes. Although it looks a little like a Yorkshire terrier, this breed is reputed to have originated entirely by cross-breeding in Australia.

CHINESE LION DOG
Another name for the Pekingese is the "Lion Dog of Peking". There is a legend that these dogs were first bred to represent the lion spirit of Buddha. Today the Pekingese, with its big eyes, round head, flat face, and soft fur looks more like a cuddly toy than a lion.

A Pekingese walks with a rolling gait, trying to distribute its weight evenly on its short legs

PEKINGESE PAIR
There have been miniature dogs in China for at least 2,500 years, but there is little evidence that the Pekingese itself is a very ancient breed. The first Pekingese dogs were brought to England after the sacking of the Summer Palace in Peking (now Beijing) in 1860, since when the breed has become smaller and more short-legged.

A POPULAR PINSCHER
The miniature pinscher is a much older breed than its bigger cousin, the Dobermann pinscher. As with the Dobermann, show standards have meant that the tail of the breed should be docked (pp. 44–45), a practice which prevents the dog from expressing its emotions correctly and upsets its balance when running.

Head is well-rounded with a turned-up nose

PAINTED POMERANIAN
In the 18th century, when the English artist Thomas Gainsborough (1727–1788) painted this Pomeranian bitch with her puppy, the breed was much larger than it is today. The Pomeranian is a miniature spitz and has the stocky body, pricked ears, ruff of fur, and curled tail that is typical of this group of northern dogs (pp. 46–47).

ROYAL FAVOURITE
Probably originating in China or Japan, this good-tempered, little dog arrived in England from France in the 16th century. It was Charles II's great fondness for this dog that gave the breed its name.

The miniature pinscher is no softy and has the strong legs of a much larger dog

King Charles spaniel

The tail of the Bichon is always curled over its back

BICHON FRISE
Within recent years the Bichon Frise (meaning "curly lap-dog") has become increasingly popular, especially in the USA. The Bichon is a Franco-Belgian breed, rather like a small poodle, and although it looks, literally, like a toy it is a lively little dog and loves a game.

The white coat has a very soft woolly underfur and an upper layer of loosely curled silky hairs

Cross-bred dogs

THE DEVELOPMENT OF BREEDS OF DOG for different purposes, like hunting (pp. 40–41), herding (pp. 42–43), guarding (pp. 44–45), or for sport(pp. 46–47), has been a long slow process that has continued over more than 5,000 years. However, most of the dogs in the world are still mongrels, or "cross-bred" dogs. These are dogs that have interbred with each other at random, as opposed to pure-bred dogs (pp. 48–59), which are dogs of the same breed that have been selectively bred by humans. It is possible for all the 400 breeds of dog in the world to interbreed because they are all descended from the wolf (pp. 8–9) and so they all belong to one species. It would be difficult, obviously from a practical point of view, for a Great Dane to mate with a tiny Pekingese. However, many unlikely crosses have occurred – like a dachshund with a German shepherd. It is often claimed that cross-bred dogs are more intelligent than pure-bred dogs, but it is more likely that their behaviour just shows more variation because they combine good characteristics of a number of different breeds.

SITTING DOG
This mongrel is eagerly waiting for its reward.

Tail arched upwards helps dog retain its balance

ONE GIANT LEAP FOR DOGKIND
These five pictures (right) show the actions used by this cross-bred dog in jumping over an obstacle. The tail is particularly important for keeping the dog's balance.

Strong, well-muscled legs help this dog to jump high off the ground at the beginning of its leap

Correct stance for getting ready for takeoff

GOOD DOG!
Training a dog to establish good behaviour patterns can be a long and arduous process, as this child realizes – but they will both get their rewards in the end.

"HIS MASTER'S VOICE"
This painting by English artist Francis Barraud (1856–1924) was bought by a gramophone company for £100. The dog, "Nipper", was the artist's own, and he was a cross-bred with a lot of bull terrier in him. This charming picture and its slogan were registered as a trade mark in 1910, and are known around the world still as a sign of a famous record company.

Strong, well-proportioned legs

ON THE DOGHOUSE
Snoopy – the world's favourite cartoon dog – is mainly a beagle with a bit of something else too. Many amusing adventures befall him each week in comic strips, but – like most dogs – he likes to sleep and dream, especially on top of his kennel.

WAITING FOR A FRIEND
A dog's wagging tail is seen as a friendly gesture towards either humans or other animals. This small figure of a pet dog, made of terracotta in 500 B.C., was found in Boeotia in central Greece.

DOGS' BEST FRIEND
This poignant painting, entitled *L'Ami des Bêtes*, by French artist Constantin Magnier was published in 1910. It shows an old tramp sharing his small amount of food with his only friends – a large group of mongrels.

KEEPING ITS COOL
This attractive cross-bred puppy (pp. 20–21) is licking its nose to help keep cool on a hot summer's day.

Bright, alert eyes

Medium-length coat – neither too short, nor too long

Tail arches over back when dog touches down

Well-defined body outline

Well-shaped nose

Front legs are straight and feet firmly on the ground when jump is completed

Pert, expressive ears

A MOTLEY CREW
These cross-bred dogs are without any extremes of physical form or function, and they will provide companionship, friendship, and loyalty for their owners. Apart from their individual endearing qualities, cross-breeds are often tougher, better-tempered, less disease-prone, and more adaptable than their pedigree counterparts.

Looking after a dog

Ownership of a dog should only be taken on by people who are prepared to keep the animal for the whole of its life – up to 17 years. For the first year, training a puppy is not very different from bringing up a child, and, in some ways, it is much easier as a dog can be house-trained much faster than a child. The dog's every need must be attended to, but at the same time it must be taught to take its place within its human family. A dog should never be left on its own for more than a few hours. It requires clean drinking water, regular meals at set times (to fit into the family's routine), and hard biscuits, or bones, to chew on, to keep its teeth clean. Every dog should be treated for internal and external parasites, such as tape-worms and fleas, and inoculated against diseases such as distemper and, in countries where it occurs, rabies.

BATHTIME FOR BONZO
This little girl is intent on keeping her pet clean.

1. Ready and waiting for a grooming session

2. A partially clipped poodle

3. Fine tuning underneath

TICKLISH TAPERING
Originally the poodle was a water dog (pp. 54–55) and its coat was clipped to stop it getting matted. Today, most poodles are companion animals, but even so the coat should be clipped for the dog's comfort rather than for showing standards.

4. Very wet poodle after its bath

5. Perfecting the tail

6. The end result

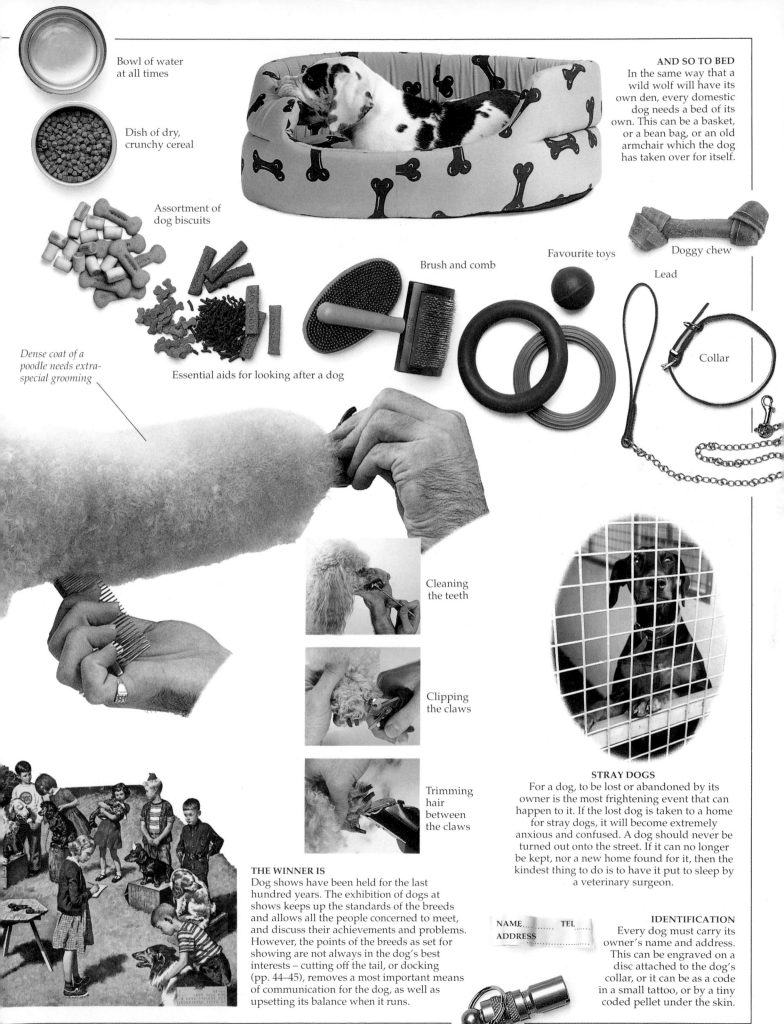

Bowl of water at all times

Dish of dry, crunchy cereal

Assortment of dog biscuits

AND SO TO BED
In the same way that a wild wolf will have its own den, every domestic dog needs a bed of its own. This can be a basket, or a bean bag, or an old armchair which the dog has taken over for itself.

Favourite toys

Doggy chew

Lead

Brush and comb

Collar

Dense coat of a poodle needs extra-special grooming

Essential aids for looking after a dog

Cleaning the teeth

Clipping the claws

Trimming hair between the claws

STRAY DOGS
For a dog, to be lost or abandoned by its owner is the most frightening event that can happen to it. If the lost dog is taken to a home for stray dogs, it will become extremely anxious and confused. A dog should never be turned out onto the street. If it can no longer be kept, nor a new home found for it, then the kindest thing to do is to have it put to sleep by a veterinary surgeon.

THE WINNER IS
Dog shows have been held for the last hundred years. The exhibition of dogs at shows keeps up the standards of the breeds and allows all the people concerned to meet, and discuss their achievements and problems. However, the points of the breeds as set for showing are not always in the dog's best interests – cutting off the tail, or docking (pp. 44–45), removes a most important means of communication for the dog, as well as upsetting its balance when it runs.

NAME....................TEL............
ADDRESS.................................

IDENTIFICATION
Every dog must carry its owner's name and address. This can be engraved on a disc attached to the dog's collar, or it can be as a code in a small tattoo, or by a tiny coded pellet under the skin.

Did you know?

AMAZING FACTS

Dogs can smell and hear better than they can see. Dogs see things first by their movement, second by their brightness, and third by their shape.

Rhodesian ridgebacks have a visible ridge, which is made up of forward-growing hairs, running along the top of their back.

A dog's sense of smell is at least a thousand times better than ours. "Scent" dogs, which have been bred to pursue other animals by their smell alone, can distinguish several different scents at the same time, and identify them as well. Dogs have 20 to 25 times more smell-receptor cells than people do.

A bitch suckling her young

Hair from some dogs, such as the Samoyed, can be spun into thread and woven into clothes.

Dogs hear much better than humans do. Dogs can hear high-pitched sounds that humans are not aware of at all. They can also hear sounds from a great distance, and can work out the direction of a faint sound.

The basenji, an African wolf dog, is the only breed of dog that is not able to bark.

Basenji

Dogs eat quickly and can regurgitate food very easily. This is useful for wolves, who are able to travel quite a long way from a kill back to their dens, where they regurgitate the food to feed their pups. It is also useful for other dogs, who get rid of bad food by being sick.

Long-faced dogs have eyes on the sides of their head, and so have a wider field of vision. Short-faced dogs tend to have eyes that are facing forwards, and so are very good at judging distances.

Big dogs tend to have larger litters than small dogs, but small dogs usually live longer than large dogs.

Bulldogs were originally bred to bait and fight bulls and bears.

Dogs only have about 10 vocal sounds, whereas domestic cats have about 20. Dogs communicate a great deal through body language – young puppies understand hand signals before words in early training.

Almost one in three families in France and the U.S. owns a dog, whereas in Germany and Switzerland there is only one dog for every ten households.

On average there are 320 bones in a dog's skeleton, but the exact number depends on the length of the dog's tail.

A dog was the first animal to go into space. In 1957, Russian scientists sent Laika, a small dog, around the earth in a satellite.

The greyhound is one of the oldest breeds of dog.

A Newfoundland dog swimming

Newfoundland dogs are strong and agile swimmers. Like many breeds of dog, they have webbing between their toes, which helps them paddle through water.

A newborn puppy is deaf for two to three weeks, until its ear canals open up.

Most puppies have 28 temporary teeth, which they begin to lose at about 12 weeks of age. They have usually grown their 42 permanent teeth by the time they are six months old.

Unlike cats, dogs cannot retract (pull in) their claws.

Bloodhounds have an amazing sense of smell. They can successfully follow scent trails that are more than four days old.

Bloodhound

A dog searching a car for drugs

Record Breakers

THE OLDEST DOG
An Australian cattle dog named Bluey lived to be 29 years and five months old.

THE HEAVIEST AND LONGEST DOG EVER RECORDED
An Old English mastiff named Zorba holds the record as the heaviest and longest dog. In 1989, Zorba weighed 155 kg (343 lb) and was 2.5 m (8 ft 3 in) long from nose to tail.

THE TALLEST BREEDS AND THE SMALLEST BREED
The smallest breed of dog is the chihuahua. However, dogs from a number of breeds can attain 90 cm (36 in) at the shoulder, and so are classed as the tallest breeds. They are the Great Dane, the Irish wolfhound, the St Bernard, the English mastiff, the borzoi, and the Anatolian karabash.

Great Dane

Q Why do the police use dogs?

A The police use dogs because of their excellent sense of smell. "Sniffer" dogs sometimes help the police to track down escaped prisoners, and also help to find illegal drugs.

Q Why do dogs chase their tail?

A A puppy instinctively chases the tip of its tail, perhaps because it resembles moving prey. If an adult dog chases its tail it is more likely to be because it has not had enough exercise, or because it has fleas, or some other medical problem.

Q Which dogs are considered the cleverest?

A Most sheepdog breeds are very intelligent and easy to train. Gundogs also respond well to training. Some of the smaller breeds, for example the poodle, are very good at performing tricks.

Q How should you approach a strange dog?

A If you have to get close to an unfamiliar dog, kneel down and let the dog come and sniff the back of your hand. Do no make sudden movements or stare into the dog's eyes, as that might feel like a threat. If the dog seems aggressive, avoid eye contact and back away slowly. Do not turn and run, as that might encourage the dog to chase you.

Q Why do dogs pant?

A Unlike people, dogs cannot cool themselves by perspiring. They only have sweat glands in their feet, and these don't have a great effect on their body temperature. But panting helps a dog stay cool. When saliva evaporates from the tongue and mouth, it helps to reduce the dog's body heat.

Q Why do dogs eat grass?

A Dogs often eat grass when they are not feeling very well. The grass makes them sick and the dogs may feel better aftterwards.

Q Can dogs see in colour?

A A dog's colour vision is limited to shades of grey and blue. The colours green, red, yellow, and orange all look the same.

Q Why do dogs' eyes glow in the dark?

A At the back of each eye a structure called the "tapetum lucidum" reflects light back into the eye, making it possible for the dog to see in dim light. When a bright light strikes a dog's eyes, it is reflected back making the eyes appear to glow.

Q What is a dorgi?

A When a dachshund and a corgi mate, their offspring are called dorgis. Famous dorgis include those born to Queen Elizabeth's corgi and the Queen Mother's dachshund.

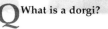

Border collies often herd sheep

Identifying dogs

Dogs come in many different sizes – from the tiny chihuahua to the giant Irish wolfhound. The Kennel Club of Great Britain recognizes more than 150 breeds of dog, and divides them into seven groups, according to the dog's role.

HEAD SHAPES

Long-headed dogs have long, often tapering noses. Round-headed breeds have a short nose. Square-headed dogs have a step between the muzzle and the forehead. It is known as the 'stop'.

A beagle has a square muzzle

The borzoi has long, powerful jaws

A pug has a very flat face

Square head   Rounded head   Long head

COAT TYPES

Short-haired dogs have a smooth coat. Most long-haired breeds have a thick undercoat with a longer coat on top. Wire-haired dogs have a short undercoat with longer, wiry hairs on top. A few breeds have a corded, felt-like coat.

Long-haired old English sheepdog

Short-haired Entelbuch mountain dog

Wire-haired Schnauzer

Hungarian puli

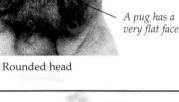

Greyhounds have excellent sight

Racing greyhounds wear a coat showing their number

HOUNDS
For a long time, people have bred dogs to help them catch other animals. Some extremely fast hounds, such as the greyhound, whippet, or saluki are "sight" hounds, which means that they chase things that they can see. Other hounds, such as bloodhounds, beagles, and bassets have great stamina and pursue by scent rather than by sight.

Dalmatian puppies are coloured pure white when they are born; their spots develop as they grow

UTILITY DOGS
This group contains a wide variety of different dogs, bred for specific functions not included in the working or sporting categories. Japanese noblemen bred the akita, for example, to help them hunt bears, wild boar, and deer. Nowadays the akita is used mainly as a guard dog. The Dalmatian was a carriage dog – it trotted along between the back wheels of a carriage in order to put off any potential attackers.

The Jack Russell terrier's coat is mainly white

TERRIERS

Terriers are alert, bold, and fearless. Most were originally farm dogs, kept as rat catchers. They love digging, and some, such as the fox terrier, were used to flush out foxes. Others, such as the Airedale terrier, hunted badgers and otters.

PASTORAL DOGS

Many dogs in this group still herd sheep and cattle today. The border collie is excellent with sheep, while the blue heeler can accurately control cattle. Herding dogs are active and intelligent. Most have a double coat, which protects them in rough weather conditions.

GUN DOGS

Gun dogs are responsive, friendly, and highly intelligent, but require a great deal of exercise. The group includes pointers, spaniels, setters, and retrievers, like this Labrador retriever. Many are good at flushing out birds for hunters and at retrieving the bird once shot. Some, such as the épagneul Picard, are particularly good at retrieving water-birds, while the Spanish water dog is excellent at retrieving game from the sea.

Chihuahua

TOY DOGS

Known also as companion dogs, breeds in this group are usually friendly and intelligent, and love attention. Most are also small in size.

WORKING DOGS

This group includes guard dogs, such as the mastiff and Dobermann, dogs to pull sledges or carts, such as the Siberian husky and the Bernese mountain dog, dogs for helping fishermen, such as the Newfoundland dog, and dogs for search and rescue, such as the St Bernard.

Find out more

ONE OF THE BEST WAYS OF FINDING OUT MORE about dogs is to spend some time with them. You could offer to walk a neighbour's dog, or simply spend some time with friends who have a dog. You could go along to one of the many different dog shows that take place all year round, and watch the competitions and training displays. Or you might consider volunteering to help the Dogs Trust or the RSPCA. Charities welcome the help of volunteers as they work to rescue and rehome injured and abandoned dogs and puppies.

Tell your puppy immediately if it has done something wrong

DOG TRAINING
The Good Citizen Dog Scheme (GCDS) runs an extensive dog-training programme up and down the country. Since its launch in 1992, over 52,000 dogs have passed the GCDS tests. The scheme provides information about basic dog training, grooming, exercise, diet, cleaning up after your dog, and healthcare. You can watch GCDS displays at major dog shows.

A dog must learn to sit obediently at its owner's heels

A PET PUPPY
If you get a puppy as a pet, it is important that you spend enough time with it while it is young. Dogs relate best to people if they start having plenty of contact as young puppies. Your dog needs clear instructions on how to behave, but also plenty of support, affection, and praise.

CRUFTS
The largest dog show in the world, Crufts takes place over four days in March each year, and has more than 120,000 visitors. Hundreds of stands promote all the things you might need for your pet, and there are many competitions and displays. More than 20,000 top pedigree dogs compete for the sought-after award of "Best in Show".

Crufts BEST IN SHOW
Pedigree

Crufts RESERVE BEST IN

HELP DOGS IN TROUBLE
Consider helping the Dogs Trust or the Royal Society for the Prevention of Cruelty to Animals (RSPCA), either with your time, or by fund raising. Both these charities rescue animals that are abandoned or badly treated and find new homes for them.

An RSPCA officer comforts a scared dog

The assistance dog provides warmth and affection as well as practical help

HELPFUL DOGS
Well-trained dogs can be a huge help to people who are physically disabled. The dogs open and close doors, pick up things that have been dropped, turn lights on and off, go for help, and provide constant love and companionship. Find out more about charities such as Dogs for the Disabled or Hearing Dogs for Deaf People, and see how you can help.

Places to Visit

CRUFTS, BIRMINGHAM, ENGLAND
• Crufts takes place in March each year at the National Exhibition Centre in Birmingham. In addition to the vast range of competitions and displays, there are over 400 trade stands and it is possible to find out about more than 180 different breeds of dog. To find the exact dates and all the latest details, go to
www.crufts.org.uk

DISCOVER DOGS, LONDON, ENGLAND
• This show, organized by the Kennel Club in London in November each year, enables visitors to find out about owning a dog, and about the many different breeds. Contact the Kennel Club for details about the dates, location, and all the latest information.

TRING MUSEUM, HERTFORDSHIRE, ENGLAND
• A display of mounted dogs demonstrates how breeds have altered over the years. Breed dogs donated to the museum in the early years of the last century look substantially different from the same breeds today.

LEEDS CASTLE, MAIDSTONE, KENT, ENGLAND
• The castle exhibits an interesting collection of dog collars through the ages.

A dog collar from the collection at Leeds Castle

AGILE DOGS
By going to dog shows you will find out a lot more about what dogs can do. Some shows include agility competitions, in which dogs jump fences, weave through poles, cross see-saws, and go through tunnels, as well as jumping onto tables and lying immobile for a few seconds before continuing. Owners run around the course directing their dog. The winner is the fastest dog with the least penalties for knocking down fences, or missing parts of the course.

USEFUL WEBSITES

• For details about the Kennel Club and its many activities, see
www.the-kennel-club.org.uk/
The website includes sections on the Young Kennel Club (YKC), a club for young dog lovers, and on the GCDS dog-training scheme.

• For full coverage of the Crufts dog show, go to
www.the-kennel-club.org.uk/crufts/cruftsframe.asp

• To obtain details of dog-training clubs in your area, see
www.dogclub.co.uk/site/index.php

• For information about the work of the Dogs Trust and its rehoming centres, go to
www.dogstrust.org.uk/

• To find out about the RSPCA, get information about their rehoming service, or for advice on owning a dog, see
www.rspca.org.uk/

• For a comprehensive listing of dog rescue centres throughout the UK, see the Dog Rescue Pages on
www.dogpages.org.uk/

• Find out about the Cinnamon Trust, a charity that arranges for volunteers to walk the dogs of elderly people who are unwell, at
www.cinnamon.org.uk

• For information on breeders, go to
www.ukdogs.co.uk

St Bernard

Glossary

Beagles have drop ears

BAIT Something edible put out to attract animals.

BAT EARS Erect ears that are wide at the base, rounded at the tips, and point out.

BITCH An adult female dog.

BREED A group of dogs with particular characteristics. Humans control breeding to achieve specific features, such as coat type or head shape. If the breeding is not strictly supervised, characteristics can very quickly be lost.

BREEDING The process of producing animals by mating one animal with another.

BREED STANDARD The official description of a breed, setting out size, weight, colour, etc.

BRINDLE A mix of tan and black hair.

An Italian greyhound bitch with her puppies

BRUSH A term used to describe a bushy tail; also a fox's tail.

CAMOUFLAGE The coloration of an animal that either blends in with the colour of the surroundings or breaks up the animal's outline with stripes or spots, making it harder to see. Camouflage can be important both for animals that hunt and for those that are hunted.

CANID A member of the dog family. The term comes from *canis*, which is the Latin word for dog.

CANINE Dog or doglike; it is also the large tooth between the incisors and the premolars, used for gripping prey.

CARNIVORE A member of the order Carnivora – which contains animals that have teeth specialized for biting and shearing flesh. Most carnivores live primarily on meat.

CLASS Any of the taxonomic groups into which a phylum is divided. A class contains one or more orders. Dogs are part of the class Mammalia.

CROP The removal of the top of the ears so that they stand upright, and are pointed rather than rounded at the tip. Cropping the ears is illegal in some countries, including Great Britain.

CROSS-BREED An animal whose parents are from different breeds, or who are themselves cross-breeds.

DEN The retreat or resting place of a wild animal.

DEW CLAW The claw on the inside of the legs. It is not used for any particular purpose.

DEWLAP The loose folds of skin hanging under a dog's throat, as in the bloodhound.

DOCK The shortening of a tail by cutting.

DOG Specifically an adult male dog, but used in a general way for all dogs, regardless of age or sex.

DOGGY PADDLING To swim moving your limbs in vertical circles, the way that a dog swims.

DOMINANT The animal that is stronger and in a more powerful position in a group.

DOUBLE COAT A coat made up of a soft, insulating undercoat, through which longer guard hairs protrude.

DROP EARS Ears that hang down, close to the sides of the head.

ECOLOGICAL NICHE The position and role of a plant or animal within its community, including all the ways in which it interacts with other living things.

ERECT Standing upright.

FAMILY Any of the taxonomic groups into which an order is divided. A family contains one or more genera. Canidae is the name of the dog family.

FERAL DOGS Domestic dogs that have returned to living in the wild and now live totally outside human control.

FORELEGS The front legs of a four-legged animal.

GENUS (plural **GENERA**) Any of the taxonomic groups into which a family is divided. A genus contains one or more species.

GROOM To rub down, clean, and smarten up a dog.

GUARD HAIRS The coarse hairs that form the outer coat of some mammals.

GUN DOGS A group of dogs trained to work with a hunter or gamekeeper, at pointing, flushing out, and retrieving game.

HACKLES The hair on the back and neck, which is raised when a dog is frightened or in order to show aggression.

HINDLEGS The back legs of a four-legged animal.

Labradors are gun dogs

HOUNDS A group of dogs used for hunting, including fast but lightly built "sight" hounds, and stocky but relentless "scent" hounds.

JAWS The part of the skull that frames the mouth and holds the teeth.

LIGAMENT The tough tissue that connects bones and cartilage, and that supports muscle.

LITTER A group of puppies born at one time to one female.

Three cross-breed dogs, or mongrels

MONGREL A dog of mixed or unknown breeding. Also known as a cross-breed.

MOULT To lose hair so that new growth can take place. Dogs moult particularly in the spring when they lose the thick coat they had for the winter.

MUSCLE Tissue that can contract or relax and as a result allow movement.

MUZZLE The part of the head that is in front of the eyes.

OLFACTORY Relating to the sense of smell.

ORDER Any of the taxonomic groups into which a class is divided. An order contains one or more families. Dogs belong to the order Carnivora.

PACK A group of animals of the same kind. The animals usually live together, may be related, and hunt cooperatively.

PEDIGREE The record of a pure-breed dog's ancestors.

PHYLUM A major taxonomic division of living organisms. A phylum contains one or more classes. Dogs belong to the phylum Chordata, which includes animals that have backbones (known as vertebrates).

PUPPY A dog that is less than one year old.

PURE-BREED A dog whose parents belong to the same breed. Also known as a pedigree dog.

REGURGITATE To throw up food that has been eaten. Wolves and other hunting dogs do this to feed their young.

RUFF Long, thick hair around the neck.

SADDLE Black markings in the shape and position of the saddle on a horse.

SCALE OF DOMINANCE The order from the most powerful to the least powerful animal in a group.

SCAVENGER An animal that feeds on other animal remains that it steals or finds.

SCENT HOUND A dog that has been bred to use its excellent sense of smell more than its sight or hearing when pursuing other animals. Bloodhounds, beagles, and foxhounds are scent hounds.

SIGHT HOUND A dog with excellent sight that will chase game while it can see it. Greyhounds, Afghan hounds, and borzoi are sight hounds.

SKELETON The framework of bones that gives shape to an animal, provides anchorage for muscles, protects vital organs, is a source of blood cells, and provides a mineral store.

SPECIES Any of the taxonomic groups into which a genus is divided. Members of the same species are able to breed with each other.

SPITZ Any of various breeds of dog characterized by a stocky build, a curled tail, a pointed muzzle, and erect ears. The chow chow is a spitz.

STEREOSCOPIC VISION The ability to see a slightly different picture with each eye, and, by putting them together, to judge distances accurately.

STUDBOOK The book in which breeders register the pedigrees of dogs.

SUCKLE To suck milk from the mother. The term also means to give milk to a young animal.

TAPETUM LUCIDUM The cells at the back of a dog's eye that reflect light. The tapetum lucidum makes it possible for a dog to see well when there is not a lot of light.

TAXONOMIC Relating to the classification of organisms into groups, based on their similarities or origin.

TENDON A band of tough tissue that attaches a muscle to a bone.

TERRIERS A group of active, inquisitive dogs originally trained to hunt animals living underground.

THIRD EYELID Situated inside the upper and lower eyelids, this thin fold of skin can be drawn across the eye, protecting it from dust and dirt.

TICKED A coat in which spots of colour stand out against the background colour.

TOY DOGS A group of very small dogs popular as pets.

Yorkshire terrier

UNDERCOAT (or **UNDERFUR**) The dense, soft fur beneath the outer, coarser fur in some mammals.

UTILITY DOGS A varied range of different dogs that are useful to humans in one way or another.

WEAN To cause a puppy to replace its mother's milk with other food.

WHELP A puppy that has not yet been weaned and is still feeding on its mother's milk. The term also means to give birth to puppies.

WORKING DOGS A group of dogs that work for people, for example, by pulling sleds, herding sheep, or guarding buildings.

Puppies playing

Index

Acknowledgements

Dorling Kindersley would like to thank:
Trevor Smith's Animal World, V Battarby, R Hills, E Mustoe, H Neave, D Peach, R Ramphul, S Renton, S Surrell, J Williamson, and J Young for lending dogs for photography.
The zoos of Augsburg, Duisburg, and Osnabrück for providing wild dogs for photography.
J Larner for grooming section.
The British Kennel Club and Mrs R Wilford for breed information.
The Natural History Museum's staff and R Loverance of the British Museum for their research help.
J Gulliver for her help in the initial stages of the book.
C Carez, B Crowley, C Gillard, T Keenes, and E Sephton for their editorial/design assistance.
J Parker for the index.
Illustrations:
E Sephton, J Kaiser-Atcherley

Picture credits
The publisher would like to thank the following for their kind permission to reproduce their

photographs:
a=above t=top b=bottom c=centre l=left r=right
Advertising Archives: 60bl, 63bl
Allsport: 46cl; /Bob Martin: 15cr
American Museum of Natural /
  A E Anderson: 9tl; /Logan: 9ct
Ancient Art and Architecture Collection: 49bcl
Animal Photography/Sally Anne Thompson: 39tr, 45tr, 45br, 50c
Ardea, London Ltd/Eric Dragesco: 25tl; /Ian Beames: 35br; /John Daniels 68c, 69bl; /Jean-Paul Ferrero: 22t, 37cl, 56c; /Kenneth W Fink: 20bl, 31br; /M Krishnan: 36cbl; /S Meyers: 28tl
Australian Overseas Information Service, London: 37tr
Bridgeman Art Library: 6tl, 6–7t, 7tr, 40cl, 41tl, 41tr, 42tr; Cadogan Gallery, London: 18cl; Oldham Art Gallery, Lancs: 46tr; Rafael Valls Gallery, London: 55bl
British Museum: 34tl, 34br, 35cl, 35bl;
  Museum of Mankind: 26br
Jean-Loup Charmet: 19bl, 51bl, 58cr, 61tr
Bruce Coleman/John M Burnley: 19tl; /Jessica Ehlers: 36bl; /Jeff Foott: 32cl; /Gullivan & Rogers: 33br; /F Jorge: 32tr; /Leonard Lee Rue: 25tc, 29tl
Columbia Pictures Television: 39tl
Corbis: 64–65 (background) /Gallo Images 25crb /Richard Hamilton Smith 67b /Kevin R Morris 67cr /Tom Nebbia 64tr, 69c /Rick Price 66–67

(background) /Ariel Skelley 68tr /Greg Smith 65tl /Dale C Spartas 67cl
Sylvia Cordaiy Photo Library: 63cbr
Cyanamid (UK)/Animal Health Div: 11b
C M Dixon: 36tl
DK Images: Tracy Morgan 64bl, 65cr, 66clb, 66bl, 66cbl, 67tl, 68–69 (background), 70t, 70cl, 70b, 70–71 (background)
EMI Records: 60cr
English Heritage/Keith Hobbs: 52cr
e.t. Archive: 48bl
Mary Evans Picture Library: back jacket cl, 10tl, 16bl, 21c, 22cb, 44bl, 47bl, 48tl, 48tr, 53tc
Marc Henrie, ASC (London): 42br
© Hergé: 47cr
Michael Holford: front jacket br, 4br, 34bl, 38cl, 58bl
Hutchison Library/H R Dörig: 32tl; /R Ian Lloyd: 35tl
ILN Picture Library: 53cl, 56br
Image Bank: 12tl, 30tl
Imperial War Museum: 44tr
Kennel Club Picture Library: 68b
Dave King: 10br, 13ctl, 39 br, 42 bl, 45cr, 48cl, 51tl, 52tl, 52–53t, 53cr, 54tr, 54bl, 57tl, 61bl
Kobal Collection: 42tl; /Avco Embassy: 23br; /Twentieth Century Fox: 49tl
Michael Leach: 29cb
Leeds Castle: 35bc, 69cr
Macmillan Inc: 8br

National Archive of Canada/ Karen E Bailey (C–137830): 57b
National Portrait Gallery: 56tr
Natural History Museum Pubs: 9br
Peter Newark's Pictures: 25c, 29cr
NHPA/Michael Leach: 36ctl; /Mandal Raijit: 27bl
Robert Opie Collection: 44tl, 50tl, 54cr, 62tl
Oxford Scientific Films/O Newman: 23cr
Planet Earth Pictures/J R Bracegirdle: 24bc; /Jim Brandenburg: 11cr, 23bl; /J Scott: 21tl
Axel Poignant Archive: 36br
Retrograph Archive/Martin Breese: 14tr, 20tl, 42cl, 44br, 46tl, 50cl, 53cr
Reuters/Andy Muller 66cr
RSPCA Photolibrary/Paul Herrmann: 69tl
Gary Santry: 61cr
Science Photo Library/John Sanford: 8tl
South American Pictures/Tony Morrison: 33bl
Tate Gallery: 59tr
Tring Museum: 7bl
© 1990 United Feature Syndicate, Inc: 60br
F R Valla: 35cr
V & A Museum: 29br, 56tl, 58tl
Werner Forman Archive: 23ct, 24tr, 41tc, 54tl
Zefa Picture Library: 47cl
© Dr Erik Zimen: 18ctr, 19tr, 21cl, 23tr
All other images © Dorling Kindersley